How to
Guarantee Your Child's Success

...and your own, too!

Richard W. DeHaven

MayaLand Press
P.O. Box 1260
Davis, California 95617
(916) 756-6200

Editing:	A Way With Words (Sacramento, CA)
Typing:	Quality Plus (Sacramento, CA)
Typography:	Graphic Gold (Davis, CA)
Cover Design:	Concept by the Author; Production by Graphic Gold (Davis, CA)
Printing:	Griffin Printing (Sacramento, CA)

DeHaven, Richard W. 1994
How to Guarantee Your Child's Success...and your own, too!
Self-Help/Psychology/Parenting

Library of Congress Catalog Card Number: 94-76673
ISBN: 0-9641495-0-8

Dedication

I dedicate this book to my family. And I thank each of them for putting up with me, including all my wild swings of ambition and mood, over the years.

In doing this project, I know that I've become a vastly improved person. That important change, and the techniques and principles I provide in this book, are my gifts to each member of my family. If these gifts also become the keys for them to unlock and fulfill *their* true potentials, then another of my goals will have been achieved.

Acknowledgments

"Be bold and mighty forces will come to your aid," so the saying goes. And how true this was for me in completing this project. My "mighty forces" that deserve a special thanks were...

...Marilyn Cavender, Valerie DeHaven, Susan Marks, and Darcy Millward for their accuracy and professionalism in word processing the hundreds of pages of drafts and rewrites of the manuscript.

...Marj Stuart for her editing excellence that improved the book immeasurably and taught me much new about writing.

...Kathi Zamminer and Jeanne Pietrzak for their care, patience, and professionalism in designing and typesetting the final manuscript and production of the cover.

...Penny Hancock for giving so freely of her time and advice on various aspects of the self-publishing game.

...Hoa McGraw for her valuable advice from an Oriental perspective, and for more than once helping to guide me back from the depths of procrastination.

Contents

Preface

T hank you for purchasing this book. And congratulations! You're obviously someone who wants to substantially improve either the quality of your own life or the life of someone near to you. I say congratulations because you are either taking your first—or another—giant step up the ladder to success.

I want to caution you at the onset, however. There are no overnight miracles. If you are prone to believing the flowery ads that say your financial freedom or personal success can be had for the asking in a few days or weeks, and if you are expecting the same from this book, forget it.

The concepts, principles, and very specific techniques given in this book are proven. They *will* work for you, your child, and anybody else.

But success is not simply free for the taking. It requires work and commitment. It may mean that all or part of the book will have to be periodically reread. Certain key parts may have to be studied and practiced many times, until all of the details are firmly entrenched in your mind and can be recalled automatically and subconsciously, as needed.

I hope, however, that I'll do my job so well that you won't treat this work as a chore but as a joy! We can both have some fun along the way.

As a preface to our involvement together, consider the fact that the great majority of our population live their entire lives by what one wise observer has called the "Law of Accidents." Those living under this umbrella believe that "it's not *what* you know but *who* you know that counts" and that any adversities we encounter are because "that's the way the cookie crumbles" or because "what goes around comes around."

Such people generally have no goals, make no plans, and hope that everything turns out okay for them. You are already stepping away from this crowd, with your foot on the next rung.

So ... let's get started.

Introduction

What Is Success?

A book about success should start by defining the term, right? Right!

A clear, succinct definition of success can be stated, right? Wrong!

For purposes of this book, the definition of success is bounded only by the limits **you** set. What is it that **you** really want for yourself and your children?

Do you most desire...

✧ To obtain a new job or career, or improve an existing one?

✧ Total financial freedom—no further worries about money, with the ability to travel and buy whatever you want?

✧ A brand new home, all paid for, or a Mercedes Benz in the driveway, or a sleek new sailboat docked at the local marina?

✧ To achieve some particular goal or dream, other than financial freedom, that until now you've thought impossible?

✧ Peace of mind, including freedom from negative emotions such as fear, anger, and guilt?

✧ To finally break from negative and destructive habits involving drugs, alcohol, smoking, or sex?

✧ Feelings of personal fulfillment or satisfaction for some major accomplishment?

✧ The ability to engage in loving, intimate, mature relationships—rather than dysfunctional ones—with others, especially your family?

✧ Worthy goals, ideals, and beliefs?

✧ An intimate understanding of *why* you or your child— or other family member or friend—is the kind of person they are today?

✧ To understand the reasons for, and then to rid yourself of, the guilt you have because of the way a child or other family member has turned out?

✧ High levels of energy and excellent health?

These are examples of the many ways in which you can define success. Pick from among these or develop your own definition and purposes as you read and work through this book.

Remember that success is basically no more than the progressive realization of a series of goals that are worthwhile and sought by an individual. And also remember this: Success is *not* how well you may do competing against others; more importantly, it's how well you do compared to what **you** yourself are **capable** of doing and achieving.

What Can This Book Do For You?

My mission is to give you a new pair of glasses by which to see the world. Although that world will still be exactly the same, you'll very soon begin to *see* it much differently.

Your new glasses will have a very powerful prescription. They'll magnify and multiply all of the opportunities that pass before you—daily, weekly, monthly.

The main goal of this new prescription is to help you to ensure your child's success in life. But the techniques and principles can't be learned and practiced without also benefitting the parent. In fact, the methods need not be learned and applied to your child at all. The goal can be to ensure the success of *anyone* capable of reading and comprehending the pages that follow.

And age is definitely not a barrier. It may be true that, for certain older persons, some key opportunities may be forever lost. But most of the techniques and principles we will explore can bring significant, gratifying results to even the oldest reader.

You need only *believe*. Believe that it's never too late to start on the first day of the rest of your life.

One qualifier must be added. The methods and techniques given in this book cannot be used to resolve the problems of the deeply disturbed or mentally ill child or adult. For those individuals, the services of a professional counselor or a medical specialist should be sought.

What Perspective Do I Bring?

Here is what I think is relevant of my own story. I'm from a somewhat dysfunctional family of six. The children included two boys and two girls.

Compared to my brother and two sisters, I achieved greater success during early adulthood. A college degree, a great job, and a wonderful wife all seemed to come with ease, and at a relatively early age. I attribute at least some of my good fortune to the beneficial result of being my parents' first child.

But following comparatively high achievements and successes during my 20s and early 30s, a period of homeostasis, and even some back-stepping, set in. My major problem was with debilitating addictions.

I gradually began to realize that I would never gain the financial independence that I wanted because of the way I was living and working. I knew I must find a plan, a formula, a scheme of things, that I could follow to reach greater success. So I set out to identify the important formulas and keys to success. This book represents the culmination of my search for that essential knowledge and information.

Here are a few more points to help you fully understand my perspective. First, I devoted over 18 years of my adult, professional life to research. The subject of that research is, I believe, irrelevant. But what *is* relevant is that over this period I developed skill in scientific methodology, while testing, analyzing, and compiling the results of my own and other researchers' work.

Second, I have a penchant for always seeking the facts, the "bottom line," the real "meat" of an issue or problem. I have no patience for unstructured meetings or vague and untested theories and hypotheses. I like to stay on target and keep the subject matter useful and beneficial.

A recent test I took was supposed to (and I believe did) show the general kind of "tool kit" I possess as an employee and worker. The results indicated that I like to (a) integrate and know why, (b) know both the significance and the details, (c) diagnose and solve problems, (d) have documentation for my beliefs, and (e) learn from repetition and established procedures and systems.

That's it in a nutshell. As you can see, I'm basically a "nuts and bolts" person. And that's the perspective I intend to give you throughout this book.

If you can read and follow a simple road map, you can easily follow the methods I present. And you can thereby guarantee your child's success... and your own, too.

Where Did The Information Originate?

It may be apparent by now that I was not involved in conducting the original research which has led to this book. I have merely compiled, assimilated, and condensed the findings of the world's best research studies on human performance and achievement. These studies involved dozens of researchers and thousands of research subjects over the past few decades. *All* high-achieving, successful people use the methods I cover.

You could do just what I have done by buying and assimilating dozens of self-improvement books or tapes. This would cost you hundreds or even thousands of dollars. Then there's the amount of time it would take you to wade through the speculative, untested, and unproven aspects which are invariably intertwined with the proven results.

Why bother? I've screened out the best from the rest, and it's waiting for you to assimilate in the following pages.

How Can You Best Use This Book?

As I explained in the Preface, there's no free lunch to be had here. Hard work and commitment are essential. Study and practice may, at times, be needed, as well as rereading key parts of the book.

You have spent years becoming the person that you are right now. Changing how you view things, so that the door to success for you or your child is permanently opened, may not come easily or quickly. But with patience and effort, change *will* come. Believe it!

I've incorporated three approaches to help you retain what you're reading.

First, I use brief "sayings," which are usually no more than 10 to 20 words each. I have strategically placed them near important points to help you remember the points.

Visualize these sayings as coat hooks. Each little hook can hold a lot of clothing—the key points of the book. If you remember and use the "hooks," you'll be amazed at how easily you recall the broader points of the book.

The second aid to recall is the section of stories at the end of the book. Like the sayings, they help you remember the broader principles or concepts. Telling these stories to your child will embed the points in both your minds.

A third, very important enhancer for your recall is the brief Highlights at the beginning of each significant section. Go back and reread specific Highlights as needed. You can reread all of the Highlights in one 20 to 30 minute sitting for a quick refresher of all of the significant points. In combination with the "hooks" provided by the sayings and stories, that may be all the reiteration that you will ever need.

In addition to these three simple aids for enhancing your recall ability, I've included descriptions of several games that can be played within your own family to practice and permanently instill the principles.

Will The Methods Work For You?

As a practical person, I feel an obligation to let you ask one simple question at the onset: "Will this book *really* work for me?"

Yes! I firmly and genuinely believe so. Just as the techniques, principles, and concepts within this book worked for me, they *will* work for you. I wrote, self-published, and am now successfully promoting and marketing this book, despite the years I spent on a downward spiral due to compulsive, often debilitating, addictions.

The whole book project was brought to fruition in 6 months, once I really directed myself to the goal using the methods I describe. I could not have done it without these methods, and because they are so powerful, I know they *will* also work for you.

Without exception, all top achievers worldwide practice and use these same techniques, principles, and concepts, or close approximations. There's absolutely no reason why your child's and your own success, regardless of how you define it, cannot be achieved with the same methods.

All you need is the right attitude. First, *believe* that the methods will work. And second, commit to applying the methods until they *do* work.

Don't let the potential obstacles in your path deter your resolve in any way. Your *attitude* is the key, not your training, experience, or other status.

Consider, for example, that exhaustive studies have failed

to show any relationship between adulthood wage earnings and grades in school (high school or college). Consider, for example, that up to 94 percent of top executives attribute their overall success to *attitude*, not training.

I'm convinced these methods will work for you. Take your time—up to 1 full year if you want—to assimilate and apply the techniques and methods in this book. If you're not completely convinced by then that these are universal keys to superior human performance and success, write me a letter (MayaLand Press at the address on inside cover). I'll send you a full and prompt refund of the purchase price of the book, but I'll let you keep the book as compensation for your trouble. Do we have a deal?

PART ONE:

We All Have The Same Chance—Don't We?

CHAPTER 1

We All Have The Same Chance—Don't We?

I can't recall the exact words, but I remember well the gist of the discussion. Here stood four relatively successful young adults—my wife and I, a coworker and his wife—in the kitchen of their house. At the time, three of us worked for governmental agencies.

As dinner simmered on the stove and the level in the wine bottle diminished, the discussion turned to welfare.

"Damn," Brad said, "I can't believe the amount of our tax dollars going for welfare! They should make those slime-balls work just like the rest of us."

"Yea," I agreed. "I busted my butt every inch of the way to get through college and to where I am. There's no reason every one of those welfare recipients can't do the same."

"We all have exactly the same chances in life in this country," I continued. "I say give 'em some job training and maybe 3 years of assistance, maximum. Then, if they're not functioning independently and self-sufficiently, cut them the hell off of public assistance!"

Thinking back now on that discussion more than 20 years ago embarrasses me and bolsters even more my realization of the wisdom which comes with education... and yes, with aging.

Back then, I lacked the knowledge and wisdom to

understand that we don't, unfortunately, all reach the various milestones of our chronological development with the same chances for *future* success. For me, this important understanding came gradually over the years.

My thinking evolution was triggered by events and facts too lengthy and complex to discuss here. But a few recent news items illustrate some of the key points and recurring issues. These are some of the more *extreme* examples of why we don't all have equal chances for achieving success.

Let's relive for a few moments these recent (and perhaps familiar) news flashes:

FLASH: ROBERT ALTON HARRIS, KILLER.

Since killing two San Diego teenagers in 1978, Robert Alton Harris was confined on death row at California's San Quentin Prison. As a dirty yellow dawn rose over the prison on April 21, 1992, he became the first person executed by this state in 25 years.

Part of the vengeance against Harris stems from the despicable nature of his crimes. In 1975, as an adult of 22, Harris savagely beat a man to death, despite the man's pleas that he stop.

The 1978 victims—John Mayeski and Michael Baker—had the misfortune of stopping for hamburgers at Jack-in-the-Box across from the San Diego Trust and Savings Bank. Nearby, Robert Harris and his brother were casing the bank and looking for a car to steal in preparation for a robbery.

Mayeski and Baker were abducted and ordered to drive to a nearby fire trail. Robert Harris then directed them to walk up a hill where Mayeski was shot to death. As Baker prayed for his life, Harris leaned over him before firing the fatal shots and sneered, "God can't help you now, boy."

As if to underscore the callousness of the crimes,

Robert Harris then ate the boys' still-warm hamburgers. At the penalty phase of his trial, he said, "There was no thought at all in my mind, just like I was a robot... just like I was empty inside."

Was this empty robot-man a product of *his* environment? Were the abuses done *to* Robert Alton Harris any less despicable and callous than those he went on to commit?

Consider Harris' life history and judge for yourself:
1. Harris' mother drank heavily while pregnant with him.
2. His premature birth, at 3 pounds, 14 ounces, was triggered by his father who, during a drunken, jealous rage, kicked his mother in the stomach.
3. Harris became one of nine children of Kenneth Albert Harris, an alcoholic Korean War veteran who went to prison twice for sexually abusing one of his daughters. His mother, Evelyn Harris, was convicted of bank robbery in 1977. Over the years, turbulence reigned in the Harris household.
4. Harris' father required the family to wait nightly at the dinner table for him until he arrived home, usually drunk. As a small child, Robert Harris once fell asleep waiting and suffered the consequences. Harris' sister, Barbara Harris, later testified, "He hit him in the back of his head and his high chair fell over. Robbie fell out and was in convulsions, and there was blood coming out of his mouth, nose, and ears. Daddy said, 'Oh, look, Evelyn, your baby is bleeding to death.' He grabbed the tablecloth and started strangling him."
5. Harris and several brothers later toiled in the cotton fields of South Carolina. The abusive father more than once rebuked them as "dumb grunts" and beat them into unconsciousness.
6. When the parents finally divorced in 1963, Harris led

a nomadic existence with his mother and other siblings. Home was often a car or tent in the fruit orchards of California, Oregon, and Washington.
7. Not surprisingly, numerous juvenile facilities and penitentiaries eventually became Harris' main family and home.

FLASH: THOUSANDS OF RUNAWAYS LIVING ON THE STREETS.

Take any large city in America and a consistent picture emerges: homeless adults and kids living in the streets.

San Francisco statistics give an idea of the scope and breadth of the problem:

- ✧ *Since 1984, more than 15,000 runaways were either reported or booked by police.*
- ✧ *Within 1 week of arriving in San Francisco, almost all runaways are introduced to prostitution and drug addiction.*
- ✧ *The average age used to be 14, 15 or 16, but now that's shifting downward to 12 and 13.*

The problem in California is staggering: 20,000 to 25,000 runaways at any given time, and close to 400,000 annually. Multiply these figures by the number of states, and you can see the magnitude of the problem.

Given the lives these runaways are usually forced to lead, plus the abuses many are running *from*, can we speculate on *their* chances for success? Sure, many will eventually succeed, but their *chances* are undeniably diminished. And for those who do succeed, the road through time may be a long one.

FLASH: A TRUCK USED AS A TORTURE CHAMBER.

Authorities in El Dorado County, California, arrested a mother and father for crimes of child abuse almost too despicable to believe.

Carolyn N. Phillips, a county deputy district attorney, relates that the wife's descriptions of what her husband did, including an allegation of vampirism, make the case "one of the worst I have ever seen."

Apparently, the children—ages 6, 4, 3, 1 and 4-month-old twins—were kept confined within a rotting old pickup-camper at a local campground for almost 3 years.

The screams and cries that neighbors heard coming from the camper were believed the result of the husband's torturing the children. Often, after the father sexually molested the eldest boy, the mother would hold the child down while the father slashed the boy's buttocks with a pair of scissors.

The mother told investigators that the father had nude photographs of her and the family. When police searched the pickup, they found close-up camera lenses, a roll of undeveloped film, pornographic videos, an electric prod, and a number of leather belts.

Don't you wonder about such parents? Certainly such heinous behavior can't be inherited. What events in these parents' lives caused *them* to so degenerate? And what about the permanent scarring of their children's lives? Are they likely to grow up mimicking their parents' behaviors?

FLASH: BABIES HAVING BABIES.

With the average American girl now sexually active at 16 and the average boy a year earlier, more than a million teenagers will become pregnant this year.

That works out to at least 3,000 young girls getting pregnant each day. It is estimated that half a million teens each year bear and keep their babies, 450,000 have abortions, and about 100,000 give up the babies for adoption.

Should we believe that these babies, and the teenagers who have them, share the same chances for success as those involved in more timely, planned pregnancies?

FLASH: CHILDREN SENTENCED TO DIE.

"The death penalty came as a real surprise to me," says Wayne Thompson. "I didn't learn about the death penalty until I was in jail."

Wayne Thompson was only 15 when he was arrested and convicted in a shooting and stabbing death. Now Wayne sits on death row in an Oklahoma prison, one of 33 death row inmates nationwide who were sent there for murder and related crimes committed before they were 18.

What kind of child commits murder? Dr. Dorothy Otnow Lewis, a psychiatry professor at a New York university, says most violent youngsters have suffered a head or nervous-system injury or have shown a history of severe psychiatric illness. She notes, "When these conditions are coupled with growing up in a family in which the youth is horribly abused or must be witness to extreme violence, it seems to create a very violent individual. I'm not even sure that being the victim of the violence is as important as seeing extraordinary family violence."

FLASH: KIDS AWASH IN A SEA OF DRUGS AND ALCOHOL.

Here are three common scenes, some variations of which play out thousands of times every day across our country:

⋄ *In Kansas City, it was just one more late-night search of an apartment in a run-down complex. As the officers hunted for rock cocaine, they were shadowed by a 3-year-old girl. They were looking for drugs, the officers told the child, because drugs* *are bad. "Drugs aren't bad," the girl responded. "Jeffrey hides cocaine in my jacket pocket." Sure enough, the officers looked in the girl's red jacket and found 20 grams of rock cocaine worth more than $2,500.*

Jeffrey's arrest brings another sobering fact. For each ten parents like him—and there are hundreds of thousands—an average of 14 children are involved. When the parents are arrested, these kids are left with other relatives or are placed in foster homes.

❖ *In Seattle, Mike is now 15. He looks like an angel. He has brown hair, freckles, and blue eyes.*

"I got high on drugs for the first time in fourth grade," he says. "I got them from my baby sitter who was 16."

"I started getting high and drinking regularly in sixth grade," he says. "I was getting drunk before school." His alcoholic blackouts began in eighth grade. He was also using hallucinogenic mushrooms and acid. Drugs became the most important thing in his life.

❖ *In Denver, Chester was always filthy when he arrived at his third grade class. His hands and face were streaked with dirt, and he had an incredible body odor—part urine, part sweat, part dirt.*

Chester eventually reported being beaten and kicked in the stomach, which may have led to his frequent escapes via wine coolers. When the principal of Chester's school visited the child's apartment, she said it was the filthiest place she had ever seen—with dirty diapers strewn everywhere (Chester had three siblings under 2 years of age). Child Protective Services eventually removed all the children from the home—for 2 days—but Chester's teachers could see that the problems never went away.

FLASH: DIVORCES WREAK HAVOC.

We have become a nation of divorced parents. Thirteen million children younger than 18 now reside in homes marked by divorce.

The problem is everywhere, but perhaps of greatest overall magnitude in California, where about 50 percent of all the state's children live in single-parent homes at some point. About 90 percent of children of divorced parents are brought up by their mothers.

One of the most serious consequences of divorce to children and their mothers is that it thrusts them into poverty. The typical divorced woman's income shrinks dramatically in the year following divorce. And nationally, the percentage of children living in poverty is greater for divorced than for undivorced parents.

FLASH: POLICE BACK KILLINGS OF KIDS.

In Rio De Janeiro and other large Brazilian cities, the most final form of child abuse—extermination—is practiced. The murdering of their children has its roots in the grinding poverty, antiquated laws, family disintegration, and ineffective welfare and criminal justice systems that have deteriorated even more during Brazil's worst economic crisis.

About 12 million youngsters live on Brazilian streets today, up from 5 million in 1985. Street children usually survive first by begging or petty stealing, but later turn to bigger crimes. Storekeepers hire death squads, including retired and off-duty policemen, to "clean up" high-crime areas.

"You can get a kid under age 10 killed for $40," said one Rio police officer. "But a kid who runs drugs or heads a gang is more expensive; his head can cost up to $500."

These news highlights are just a tiny sampling of the

neglect and outright abuse to which some of our children are subjected. Admittedly, these are some pretty extreme examples.

The point is that the possibility of eventual success in life has been clearly lessened in these extreme examples. Children who are abused or neglected have lower IQs and an increased risk of depression, suicide, and drug problems. They are more likely to express severe anger, refuse to follow instructions, and lack enthusiasm. They have a greater tendency to be hyperactive, easily distracted, lacking in self-control, and disliked by their peers.

Abused children asked to relate an incident or tell a story often can't proceed from beginning to end without jumping to another story or becoming otherwise distracted. They don't seem to understand the reasons for the actions they describe. The stories they tell are often lacking in any emotion.

Abused children are more likely to grow up abusing their own children.

The list of connections goes on and on. The bottom line is simply that abuse and neglect have enormous, long-term consequences for children.

Fortunately, the ultimate effects of even the most serious child abuse are reversible to some degree. The same can be said of the less profound everyday abuses and mistakes parents—all parents—make in raising their children.

In the remaining parts of this book, my goals are to: (a) describe in more detail the common abuses and mistakes that parents are involved with; (b) show you why and how such maladies do profoundly affect us; and (c) provide you with essential tools and skills to prevent such problems from affecting you or your child in the future. It is these tools and skills which invariably provide us with a basic foundation for success.

PART TWO:

The Maladies That Limit Us

Child abuse—whether the obvious and serious kinds of trauma illustrated in Part One or the more common and subtle day-to-day parental mistakes—has serious and often long-lasting effects on a child.

These effects in turn may severely limit your child's ultimate abilities. It's important that we look more closely at these effects and resulting limitations so that we understand and better appreciate how these limitations can be controlled, reversed, and eventually overcome.

CHAPTER 2

In The Womb And Before

Highlights

✧ *A pregnant woman's use of alcohol can cause a number of debilitating effects to the unborn child, from physical abnormalities to mental retardation—Fetal Alcohol Syndrome (FAS).*

✧ *Smoking while pregnant causes problems similar to FAS.*

✧ *Drug use either before or during pregnancy can cause chromosomal changes that lead to severe birth defects and long-term behavioral problems.*

✧ *Drug and chemical use by the father before conception can affect sperm, and may thus subsequently affect the baby.*

✧ *Improper nutrition and too little weight gain by the mother during pregnancy lowers the baby's birth weight.*

✧ *Too much caffeine can cause problems in the developing fetus.*

✧ *Raising the mother's body temperature (strenuous exercise in hot weather, long hot baths) can affect the fetus and also cause premature birth.*

Untold harm occurs every year to hundreds of thousands of children while they are still in their mothers' wombs. The main offenses involve various kinds of chemical poisonings and pregnant women's poor diet. Results include children being born with everything from deformed facial features to defective brains and other organs.

To better appreciate the extreme sensitivity of the fetus during pregnancy, consider just two of many relatively recent findings. First, through ultrasound techniques, we now know that as early as 4 months after conception, a bright light shone on the mother's stomach will cause the fetus to put its hands over its eyes. Second, researchers have shown that, while in the womb, the fetus may actually recognize speech as a special sound and be able to distinguish certain spoken passages.

Speech researchers conducted a study in which they asked a group of women, beginning in their 32nd week of pregnancy and continuing until birth, to recite daily three times in succession a particular paragraph from a children's story. Three different paragraphs were used, but each mother recited only one. About 52 hours after birth, the babies were provided with special nipples and earphones. By altering their rate of sucking, they could choose to hear a woman reciting the same passage to which they were subjected while still in the womb or one of the other two passages.

"They chose the familiar story," said Anthony Casper, one of the researchers. "We're talking about recognition of linguistically relevant speech sounds," he said. "The implication is that fetuses heard, perceived, listened, and learned something about the acoustic structure of American English. What it shows is that at birth there is some knowledge of the language and culture."

Given such a high degree of sensitivity to language while still in the womb, what possible negative implications might there be? Think about it. What about the possible prenatal effect of loud noises, shouting, talking with profane language, and fighting between parents? Or what effects could there be from the parents' verbal expressions of regret over having the child?

The *possibilities* of negative effects on children in the womb are far ranging. But more research is needed before we fully understand how specific negative, prenatal verbal experiences and stimuli may affect a child's later chances for success.

When it comes to alcohol, drugs, and certain other toxic substances, however, cause-and-effect relationships that *diminish* a child's chances for success *are* firmly and clearly established.

First, consider alcohol. As recently as the mid-1960s, researchers were still concluding that drinking alcohol caused no harm to the fetus. Since then, however, more than 2,500 studies have established the connection and shown that as little as 1 to 2 drinks per day during pregnancy *can* harm the unborn baby.

One of the worst manifestations of a pregnant woman's alcohol use is referred to as Fetal Alcohol Syndrome (FAS). FAS is one of the three leading causes of mental retardation among newborns and the only one that is preventable. FAS is a group of defects that includes low birth weight, postnatal growth deficiency, malformations of the face, and various abnormalities of the body's major organs, including the respiratory system.

The most serious consequence of FAS, however, is central nervous system problems. These can include mental retardation (IQ scores may be lowered considerably), alcohol withdrawal symptoms at birth, and hyperactivity throughout childhood. The syndrome is often not detected until after the child enters school.

Researchers estimate that FAS is present in 1 to 3 of every 1,000 live births. But for every child born with full-blown FAS, up to 10 may be born with one or more alcohol-related defects. This means that more than 50,000 children a year are born with debilitating handicaps that can, and often do, limit their chances for success due to their mothers' use of alcohol during pregnancy.

The findings and related statistics due to smoking during pregnancy are no more comforting. Smoking by pregnant women causes up to 5,000 babies to be born dead each year. Pregnant women who smoke are at risk for spontaneous abortion, premature delivery, and having a low-birth-weight baby. Low birth weight is associated with all kinds of neonatal problems and deficiencies. (The average birth weight of all U.S. babies is just over 7 pounds. Generally, babies weighing less than 5 pounds at birth are lighter than nature meant them to be.)

If a woman's cigarette consumption is really high—two or more packs a day—the infant may be born mentally retarded or sustain other birth defects. Common defects are similar to those of FAS, but may include such unique facial features as small lower jaws, small mouths, and short, upturned noses.

Some evidence is even emerging that the smoking mother may increase her baby's chances of developing certain cancers. We've long known that: (a) the detrimental effects of cigarette smoke can reach across to the fetus; and (b) the fetus can change these detrimental effects into cancer-causing agents. Researchers have found that certain child-hood cancers, especially leukemia, are up to twice as likely in the offspring of mothers who smoke cigarettes during pregnancy than the offspring of those who don't.

Smoking marijuana, while not yet shown to cause serious birth defects or exhibit a possible cancer link, may be just as bad as smoking regular cigarettes. Chronic marijuana smoking appears to reduce the capacity of the lungs (about 26 percent) even more than heavy smoking of other cigarettes (about 10 percent). Babies of marijuana-smoking moms are often born underweight and have problems growing.

Researchers also believe that THC, the active ingredient in marijuana, has an effect on the pituitary gland and a number of key hormones in the mother. Because THC is fat soluble, it crosses over to and is stored in the baby's body. Exposure to THC and other chemicals is more and more being tied to physical and behavioral problems in infants.

One study of marijuana showed that women who smoked it in the second phase of their menstrual cycle had a drop in their levels of luteinizing hormone. Luteinizing hormone stimulates the ovary to produce another female hormone called progesterone, which allows the embryo to lodge in the wall of the uterus and maintain the fetus as it develops. Inadequate progesterone can: (a) prevent a woman from becoming pregnant; (b) cause spontaneous abortion by prompting the fertilized egg to dislodge; or (c) inhibit fetus development. The clearest bottom line has been expressed by Dr. Jack H. Mendelson, Harvard Medical School, who says, "Pregnant women, or women who *want* to get pregnant, shouldn't smoke marijuana."

That pregnant women shouldn't *ever* use so-called "hard" or "recreational" drugs—such as heroin, cocaine, crack, and methamphetamines—goes without saying. Drug use is of epidemic proportions today in virtually every large city in the U.S. Dangers to the unborn child include most of those that can occur with smoking and drinking alcohol during pregnancy—and even more serious problems.

Consider cocaine use by pregnant women, for example. In addition to severe behavioral problems, we're talking about likely chromosomal changes that can cause congenital abnormalities, such as ears placed too low and eyes set too far apart. Scientists believe that such babies may actually be subjected to numerous small strokes while in their mothers' wombs. This is because of the abrupt changes that occur in a pregnant woman's blood pressure due to drug usage. After birth, these babies are lethargic, almost catatonic; they often also have numerous other problems. It's hard not to agree that such children's chances for success are markedly impaired by their mothers' actions.

So far, that's what we've focused on here—the effects of chemical or drug ingestion *by the mother*. The fact that there *are* clear links to the ultimate well-being of the child is straightforward. After all, the mother and fetus are inextricably linked and intermingled via the placenta for 9 months.

But what about the other side of the equation—the father? Are there also detrimental effects due to the father's use of such drugs and chemicals prior to the baby's conception?

Researchers are just beginning to focus on this area, and to date, the answers are not as clear-cut. Nevertheless, circumstantial evidence that chemical usage can severely affect sperm is mounting. For example, marijuana lowers both sperm quantity and quality. Cigarette smokers produce sperm that have impaired ability to just get up there and fertilize. Cocaine can actually bind with the sperm without impairing its survival or mobility. But it's not yet known whether chromosomal changes, and thus birth defects, may result.

The effects of a father's heavy drinking just before conception is the newest and most surprising finding. Researchers at the University of Washington and University of Michigan found that those men who had at least two drinks daily, or at least five in one sitting during the month before conception, fathered babies who weighed an average of 6.5 ounces less than others. And this occurred whether or not the mother drank or smoked. While the cautious researchers felt it was just too early to state that this was a direct cause-and-effect relationship, the inference is certainly there. Studies of lower animals have already convincingly shown that males exposed to alcohol sire fewer, weaker, and smaller off-spring.

A detrimental co-factor often associated with chemical substance abuse in male and female parents is poor nutrition. Dietary requirements for the male to conceive a healthy fetus are largely unknown, but it makes sense that a healthy, well-rounded diet results in a healthier fetus.

On the other hand, we *do* know a great deal about the nutritional requirements of the pregnant woman, and our knowledge is expanding almost daily. For example, we know it takes about 80,000 calories to produce a healthy baby. The female body can also detect when body fat is inadequate to support the fetus' increased needs. The part of the brain called the hypothalamus temporarily turns off the secretion of pituitary hormones that control a woman's fertility when body fat drops below about 17 percent.

Once the woman does conceive, it's important that she increase her caloric intake and gain an adequate amount of weight during pregnancy—about 25 to 30 pounds. Low-birth-weight babies are usually born to women who gain less than 20 pounds. These babies have a greater incidence of malnutrition, which increases the chances of acquiring neurological damage and mental retardation.

While poor nutrition and substance abuse are among the most obvious and common causes of maladies for developing fetuses, they are by no means the only problems. New environmental risk factors and everyday behaviors which may severely harm the fetus are being identified continuously. Let's examine just a couple of these factors.

First, consider caffeine. Twenty-five years ago, we had little or no concern for a pregnant woman's intake of caffeine drinks. But recent studies have shown that as little as ½ to 1 cup of very strong coffee a day—or 3 to 4 cups of weaker coffee—can significantly increase a pregnant woman's chance of spontaneous abortion. The apparent threshold for effects is about 150 mg of caffeine a day. Coffee contains from 30 to 180 mg per cup. Tea has 10 to 110 mg per cup, while a 12-ounce can of cola has 30 to 70 mg. Even though pregnant women have been cautioned for a decade to cut down on caffeine, 90 percent still drink coffee or tea during pregnancy.

In addition to caffeine, coffee has some other worrisome substances—benzopyrene, which is known to damage fetuses, and chlorogenic acid, which is suspected of damaging genes. An adult can process about half of the caffeine out of the blood in 2½ hours, but the fetus—lacking a critical enzyme—requires from 30 to 150 hours.

Another common but sometimes overlooked risk to the fetus comes from the mother developing hyperthermia or elevated body temperature during pregnancy. This can be triggered by exercise in hot weather. However, a more common cause is hot baths or hot tubs. As soothing as these may be, and even when the mother does not feel uncomfortably hot, her core body temperature may be increased above the critical 102° mark. Such maternal hyperthermia during the first 2 months of pregnancy increases the incidence of birth defects, mainly involving brain and spinal cord development. Elevated body temperature after the fourth month can also lead to premature labor.

If a woman is pregnant or thinks she might be, she needs to stay out of hot tubs and baths, or limit the soak to 10 minutes. Australian researchers have come up with the 10-minute rule after testing the effects of 104° water on non-pregnant women (they couldn't test pregnant women; the risks to the fetuses were too great). It is important to note that the test subjects didn't feel uncomfortably hot, leading researchers to conclude that "subjective discomfort is not a reliable safeguard against overheating."

CHAPTER 3

Lack Of Touching, Nurturing, And Love

Highlights

✧ *Touch-deprived babies grow more slowly, have more ailments, and experience delays in nervous system development.*

✧ *Skin-to-skin contact with caregivers releases brain chemicals which allow babies to thrive.*

✧ *The need for skin-to-skin contact extends through adolescence and into adulthood.*

✧ *A simple hug can elevate an adult's mood and speed recovery from both illness and emotional problems.*

✧ *The amount of talking to children by caregivers sets the limits for language skill development.*

✧ *Lack of talking to children lowers their IQs.*

✧ *An increasing percentage of children are growing up without a good daily diet or the essential talking that goes with a family meal.*

✧ *When parents withhold love to force desired behavior from children—conditional love—children grow up with low self-esteem and self-image, limiting their chances for success in life.*

The lack of touching, nurturing, and loving by parents gives rise to many of the most burdensome maladies that we and our children encounter.

The classic study that introduced us to this critical area of parental behavior was conducted several decades ago. Two groups of primate infants were selected. One group received normal parental touching and nurturing, while the other group was almost totally isolated from all parental contact. The deprived babies grew slower and had more ailments than the infants who had contact with parents. The impact was so great that, before the experiment could be stopped, several of the deprived babies actually died.

Today we understand this message much more clearly. The simple experience of being touched and caressed has profound direct effects on the growth of both a baby's body and its mind.

For the first time, researchers are identifying the *neuro-chemical* effects resulting from skin-to-skin contact. In particular, the research suggests that certain brain chemicals released when the baby is touched may allow it to thrive. The absence of these chemicals, or the release of certain other chemicals in the absence of the touching, may be the cause of an infant's failure to thrive.

Every baby needs one special person to bond with. It is through this first love relationship that the baby learns about people and the world. It introduces emotions and teaches how to cope with them. This baby-love experience to a large degree governs how the next generation will be treated. Early love for the child is indeed a powerful force.

One of the most significant recent studies has found that premature infants in incubators who were simply given a gentle massage and stroking for 15 minutes three times a day gained weight 47 percent faster than other comparable babies left alone in their incubators. The infants given this touching also had signs of more rapid nervous system development, were more active, and responded more to stimuli such as a face or a rattle.

"The massaged infants did not eat more than the others," said Tiffany Field, a psychologist at the University of Miami Medical School, where the study was done. "Their weight gain seems due to the effect of contact on their metabolism."

Of added importance, however, were the results 8 months later, long after the babies' discharge. The touched infants were still doing better on tests of mental and motor skills, and still holding onto their weight advantage, compared to the premature babies not given the daily massage/stroking therapy.

As word of these findings and similar corroborating studies has spread, U.S. hospitals have slowly begun to change their policies regarding premature infant care. But incredibly, many hospitals today are still adhering to the "minimal-touch rule" and isolation booth environment that has prevailed for decades.

In contrast to the U.S. situation, we can look at other parts of the world, especially the Orient, where infant massage is much more routine. Why we should be so slow to change in the face of the strong clinical evidence showing the benefits of physical contact remains an enigma.

Physical contact is the ultimate signal to the infant that he or she is safe. Infants who are held and touched more show superior cognitive development years later, apparently because they have been more alert.

Babies who cry until they are picked up, stay cheerful while they are being held, and then cry again when they are put down, cry because they are uncomfortable without physical contact. Unfortunately, this kind of crying is often misunderstood by uninformed parents who think that the baby's crying to be picked up is an unreasonable demand that will later lead to "bad habits." In fact, just the opposite is true.

And now we're learning that the need for skin-to-skin contact extends right up through the adolescent years and even into adulthood. For instance, one recent study found that a person's blood hemoglobin is raised significantly from the warm touch of another person. Since hemoglobin carries oxygen to all parts of the body, including the brain, a simple hug can create a sense of euphoria and well-being. This in turn may speed up recovery from illness and emotional problems.

If the results of a recent university study with monkeys prove indicative, when we are deprived of loving contact as babies, we may grow up with greater long-term susceptibility to health problems. Researchers from the University of Denver separated two groups of baby macaque monkeys from their mothers for just 2 weeks. The monkeys were about 6 months old (comparable to a 3- or 4-year-old child). Later, when the monkeys were about 3 or 4 years old (comparable to a human teen), their immune systems were tested against monkeys that had not been isolated during childhood. The lonely monkeys all showed lower levels of B-cell and T-cell activity—two critical components of the body's immune system.

> ## *A little bit of affection is the best medicine on the market.*

Being with and *touching* is one of an infant's most important interactions with the parents, but *talking* to the baby follows closely. A number of studies have shown that the amount you talk to your child, especially in the second and third years of life, sets the limit on how well that child does in terms of language skills and development. A lack of talking and other related nurturing interactions between the child and parents result in decreased intelligence levels.

In one study of 158 children observed from birth to 13 years old, Brown University researchers examined a total of 10 household environmental "risk" variables that might inhibit a child's development. Such things as stressful life events, reduced family support, and lack of nurturing were included. Those children with none of the risks scored, on average, more than 30 points higher on IQ tests than children with multiple risk factors. The researchers estimated that each individual risk factor nudged the child's IQ downward by about four points.

Another similar study by the University of California at Los Angeles that began in 1972 followed a group of children from infancy through age 12. The researchers found that how the infants responded to visual stimuli, how their behavior was integrated during sleep, and how much the caregivers *talked* to the infants at home were all related to the children's intelligence levels upon entering school.

The importance of social interaction and nurturing discussion among family members is probably best illustrated during the family meal. Unfortunately, more and more children in today's society, especially those in abusive environments, have *food* but not a *family meal* prepared for them. And too many of our children receive neither a good diet nor a regular family meal. This is tragic because children are definitely oriented towards the order that comes from a calm, unrushed, socially-interactive meal. In chaotic families where these conditions are missing, the children get fragmented messages about their families and themselves. And without this valuable learning experience in social interaction, the children often have trouble interacting in society as they grow up.

What a lack of touching, nurturing, and otherwise interacting with children eventually convey to them is that they are not loved. Children who feel unloved are nearly always plagued by a sense of low self-esteem and self-image; they may also harbor related intense feelings of guilt, loneliness, and despair.

As we witness more and more the degradation of the family unit throughout the U.S. and see it being replaced by dysfunctional chaos, hundreds of thousands more of our young people are growing up not knowing or feeling the love of their parents.

Consider, for example, the work of the Reverend Robert A. Murphy of the First Baptist Church of Sacramento, California. One of his tasks is reaching out to junior and senior high students to let them know they are loved—by God and the other church members, if not by their parents.

When the Reverend Murphy asks a simple question like "What do you most want in life?" of his students, a typical range of responses includes "To get pregnant, so I'd have somebody to love" or "To be 4 years old again and have a mom and dad who love me."

> *Only one life that soon is past;*
> *only what's done with love will last.*

A lack of being loved by parents is clearly a major malady affecting our nation's children. But conditional love is almost as bad as no love. Conditional love is the giving or withholding of love to get what you want from a child. It's the manipulative "You'd better do this or mommy and daddy won't *love* you!" approach. Given the extremely serious consequences of conditional love, it's amazing that it's so widely used by uninformed parents. And that seems to be the heart of the problem—a majority of parents just don't *know* how dangerous conditional love can be.

Conditional love fosters a fear of rejection and feeling that "I have to..." These in turn often contribute to the development of the so-called Type A personality which is characterized by impatience, aggressiveness, and competitiveness and held to be associated with increased risk of cardiovascular disease.

Overall, the use of conditional love is potentially one of the most terrifying troubles of childhood. It can cause serious psychic trauma which may last well into adult life.

Maybe that was the case with Robert Henry Nicolaus, death row inmate at California's San Quentin Prison. Nicolaus managed to achieve the ignoble distinction of receiving two death penalties 23 years apart. He was first convicted of murdering his three children—Roberta, age 7; Donald, age 5; and Heidi, age 2—in 1964. He was then convicted of murdering his former wife, Heidi's mother, in 1985.

In an autobiography written from his prison cell, Nicolaus revealed that his mother had given him only conditional love. "When I was good, she was kind; when I was bad, her positive feelings towards me were summarily turned off," he said.

CHAPTER 4

Detriments Of Divorce

Highlights

✧ *Children in divorced families have a greater incidence of poor grades and behavior problems.*

✧ *IQ scores may even be lowered by divorce.*

✧ *Decline of family income and a higher incidence of poverty cause many of the problems children of divorce experience.*

R ecent studies show us that the effects of divorce on children are much more devastating and long-lasting than researchers had previously thought. It appears not to be the divorce itself that matters most, but (a) how the parents handle it, (b) whether the child is able to develop meaningful relationships with both parents, and (c) what happens to the income of the parent having custody.

Children in divorced families generally have more negative feelings about themselves, lower academic scores, more impulsiveness, more withdrawal, more problems with friendships, and more general emotional turmoil. For example, studies indicate that children of divorce are referred for psychiatric evaluation at nearly twice the rate of the non-divorced population. Other studies show more delinquent behavior and outright aggression towards parents among the children of divorce compared to children of intact homes. Some of these maladies may last years or even decades.

Behavioral changes that have been reported in preschool children following a divorce include regression in toilet training, increased irritability, more whining and crying, greater separation anxiety, and mental confusion. These children often show an inordinate need for affection, which causes them to reach out too quickly—and become more vulnerable—to unfamiliar adults.

Some new information suggests that these problems are more prevalent in boys than girls. It may simply be that boys lack the male figure to identify with in the home, since 90 percent of children of divorced parents live in the mother's custody.

The negative effects of divorce may be largely a result of the decline of income families suffer. The U.S. Census Bureau has found that children can expect to become 37 percent poorer after divorce. As a result, immediately following a divorce there are increases in the number of children living at poverty level (from 19 to 36 percent), receiving Aid to Families with Dependent Children (from 9 to 18 percent), and receiving food stamps (from 10 to 27 percent).

These are critical statistics because it has been clearly shown that persistent poverty during the first 5 years of life leaves children with IQs over 9 points lower (at age 5) than non-impoverished children. The IQ deficit appears to be the result of poverty alone and not other factors such as family structure or the mother's education level.

The effects poverty has on children's behavior is also significant. Persistently poor children are more likely to exhibit a wide array of behavioral problems.

CHAPTER 5

Failure Of The Schools

Highlights

✧ *U.S. schools do little to teach success-achieving principles.*

✧ *As a whole, the U.S. does more poorly at teaching the basics—reading, writing, and arithmetic—than smaller, less affluent countries.*

✧ *Less-demanding curricula, shorter school years, less home-work, and more TV may all contribute to U.S. school-children's poor showing in international comparisons.*

✧ *The decline of the U.S. family results in more children being ill-prepared to learn and succeed in school.*

✧ *Caring parents can learn, and then instill in their children, the techniques and principles for success.*

Certainly, our nation's schools can shoulder the blame for some of the success-limiting maladies our children are burdened with. While the schools may not be the source of most maladies per se, they all too often seem to abdicate any responsibility for teaching children to overcome them.

While working your way through this book, consider its

message relative to the U.S. school system. If you're over 30 like me, you were probably never exposed to *any* of the book's main principles, concepts, and techniques during your schooling. A few of you under the age of 30 may have been exposed to limited bits and pieces of this essential training in your schooling. If you have a child in school now, you may find even more direct, focused instruction on these basic keys to success, but exposure is still limited. Sadly, the needed curriculum changes and improvements are occurring quite slowly. Only a few scattered schools and school districts are teaching success-achieving principles such as those in this book.

> ### *If you give a man a fish, he eats for a day; if you teach a man to fish, he eats for a lifetime.*

Evidence suggests that not only do our schools often fail to teach the basic keys to personal success, but they are failing to even teach the proverbial three Rs—reading, writing, and arithmetic.

A prevailing attitude among U.S. parents, teachers, and school administrators is that our schools' problems can be resolved with two fundamental changes: spending substantially more money per pupil and reducing class sizes. But some studies have cast doubt on the potential value of such overly simplistic approaches.

For instance, some enlightening figures were recently released by the National Science Foundation and U.S. Department of Education. Their results came from worldwide testing of almost 200,000 9- and 13-year-old school children in 20 countries. The children were asked such basic questions as, "Why does the moon shine?" and "What is 23.4 minus 3.6?"

For the U.S., there was but one lone bright spot: the U.S. 9-year-old children scored near the top—but nevertheless *behind* the Koreans and Taiwanese—in the science test. However, in the other three exams, U.S. students ranked consistently near the bottom, behind the students from such countries as Korea, Italy, Scotland, Spain, Hungary, Israel, Canada, and even the former Soviet Union.

These results have challenged conventional thinking about what constitutes "quality" education. For example, the typical eighth-grade class in Korea, whose students scored highest in both math and science, holds an average of about 49 students. Contrast this to an average of 23 pupils in the equivalent U.S. classroom.

Another paradox of the study involves the relative total amounts spent on education. In the U.S., about 7.5 percent of the gross national product (GNP) goes to education, a figure exceeded by only 1 of the 20 participating countries (Israel—10.2 percent). Contrast this again to Korea, where only about 4.5 percent of the GNP goes to schooling.

Gregory Anrig, President of the Educational Testing Service, pointed to one key difference—attitude. The Korean students were applauded by their classmates when they went to take the tests, he said, while the smartest U.S. students were often labeled as "nerds" and "dweebs."

The study indicated that one of the most important determinants of performance was curriculum. The top-performing countries consistently offered a more demanding curriculum. More homework and less TV also seemed to help raise average scores.

There may also be a correlation between the U.S. children's appalling performances and the fact that they attend less school per year than children in most other nations.

U.S. students average about 175 to 180 days of school per year. In Japan, students attend 243 days a year; in Korea, 220; in Israel, 216; in Germany, 210; in Russia, 210; in Scotland, 200; and in England, 192.

The U.S. school-year calendar of from 175 to 180 days is based on an agrarian model that no longer exists in U.S. society. In other words, the children are no longer essential for helping the family to till the fields and bring in the crops.

Educational excellence may very well be increased in the U.S. if we *increase* the minimum number of school days annually for students in grades 1 through 12. This may need to be coupled with significant changes in our school curricula, including teaching the universal keys to success presented in this book.

> ## *An investment in knowledge pays the best dividends.*

Having said that and vented some of my frustration with the present U.S. school system, I want to take a closer look at our apparent teaching failures. Has U.S. educational *quality* really declined overall in recent decades, as suggested? If we look at the statistics more closely, we might have trouble supporting such a conclusion.

What we may be measuring instead with such wide-scale tests is the concurrent and steady decline of the U.S. family unit and family values. As the U.S. family has degraded, the proportion of our children with maladies that limit their capacities for learning and achieving success has increased. In other words, we may simply be sending more kids to school today who are less equipped for learning.

A recent Carnegie Foundation report shows the scope of the problem. Carnegie researchers surveyed 7,000 kindergarten teachers, the largest study of its kind. The teachers estimated that more than one-third of the nation's children—nearly 1.5 million—were ill-prepared to enter school. "The sad fact is that a vast number of children experience crippling deprivations that dramatically dampen their prospects for educational success," said the Carnegie spokesperson.

If this problem, coupled with our schools' failure to teach success-achieving methods in their curricula, isn't bad enough, consider the horrible learning environment today at many of our schools. Where sports, cheerleading, and innocent horseplay once reigned, we now have gang-banging, intimidation, and violence. Estimates vary, but as many as several hundred thousand children now bring a weapon to school every day. Each hour, at least 2,000 children are faced with a violent confrontation in or near a U.S. school.

Despite these often-handicapped learning environments, what we would likely find with closer examination of the statistics is this: Today's children from "healthy" families and backgrounds are doing just as well, if not better, than before. That should be all the more reason to learn, and then instill in our children, the techniques and principles for success, such as those given in this book.

CHAPTER 6

Low Self-Esteem/ Self-Image

Highlights

❖ *Our self-esteem and self-image can easily get distorted by how we think and act, and more importantly, by how our parents treat us during childhood.*

❖ *Low self-concept often leads to* **homeostasis,** *a desire to maintain the status quo.*

❖ *A downward spiral of overreacting to setbacks and developing emotional disability can lead to depression.*

❖ *Our feelings of lack of control keep us from taking risks that will help us up the ladder of success.*

❖ *Our fear, despair, and hopelessness drive us to the use of victim language, negative emotions, and destructive criticism.*

❖ *Destructive criticism is especially damaging to children, whose minds lack enough experience to separate truth from fiction.*

❖ *Race hatred, the lowest form of destructive criticism, is almost always a sign of low self-concept.*

U p to this point, the discussion of the maladies that limit us has laid the groundwork for considering perhaps the most serious and debilitating malady of all: **low self-esteem**.

There may be as many definitions for self-esteem as for success. But for our purposes, let us say that self-esteem is the deep feeling of one's own worth; it's how good we *feel* about ourselves, and it's a basic mental condition.

High self-esteem allows us to appreciate and accept our own worth, be accountable for our actions, and act responsibly and encouragingly to others. High self-esteem guarantees an individual is able to get along with the maximum number of people and look for the "good" in every situation.

High self-esteem means that we really like who we are in terms of our personality, job, behaviors, values, and our everyday interactions with other people. The more we like ourselves, the better we will perform in all areas. High self-esteem should not be confused with vanity, bullishness, arrogance, or false pride; these undesirable traits always overshadow a person's true self and identity, usually masking a feeling of shame. An arrogant person, especially one who puts others down, almost invariably has low, not high, self-esteem.

A trait closely related to and often viewed as either a sub-part of or another term for self-esteem is **self-image**. For this discussion, I'll define self-image as how we see our own bodies in our mind's eye. In other words, it's the concept we have of our own *physical* appearance. Do we view ourselves as fat, ugly, or otherwise unappealing, regardless of what our scales, mirrors, friends, and family tell us?

You might be surprised at how many truly attractive, healthy people have a distorted view of their own physical appearance—a low self-image. For example, 45 percent of women in one study who were *under*weight by medical standards actually saw themselves as being *over*weight. Another study found that over half of a group of 10-year-old schoolgirls each saw herself as the least attractive girl in the whole class.

What makes such distortions so cruel is that self-image and its larger counterpart, self-esteem, are so crucially linked. Dislike of our own bodies makes it difficult, if not impossible, to like ourselves and have healthy self-esteem.

This point has been referred to repeatedly by Gloria Steinem, the well-known feminist leader. She has explored her personal experiences with low self-image and self-esteem in a number of interviews, articles, and books. "Feelings of disrespect for our unique selves get internalized," she observes. "The result is a poor self-image of body and mind."

She goes on to describe how her father, who weighed more than 300 pounds, organized his whole life around food. The emotional connections between father and daughter always occurred over copious amounts of food, after which he often fell asleep—totally sedated. Years later, as an adult, Gloria finds herself a foodaholic, too; she can rarely keep food in the house without eating it, and she must stay healthy one day at a time.

She never questioned the way she *thought* she looked until one day, in her 30s, when she viewed herself on TV. What she *saw* for the first time was a thin, pretty, blond woman of medium height who spoke in somewhat of a monotone, but nevertheless confidently. What she *felt* like was a too-tall, too-plump, pudding-faced brunette, with a voice on the verge of emotional breakdown. Because of this mind's-eye picture of herself as being enormous in size, she tended to hide her face and stand round-shouldered.

Her mother, whose problem was depression, also profoundly affected Gloria's view of her own body. As a child, she connected her mother's perpetually sad heart with soft maternal hips and breasts. As a result, and to gain distance from her mother's fate, Gloria always longed for a more slender, boyish body.

A distorted view of breasts also played a role in the life

of one of Gloria's friends. This woman saw herself with such shameful, distorted breasts that she wanted to have surgery. Then, just a few days before the operation, she remembered how her grandmother had made her wear painful bindings as a developing girl. She suddenly realized that surgery would not provide the healing she needed.

Gloria Steinem and her friend are among the lucky ones. They have each identified some of the roots of their low self-image and self-esteem. This has enabled them to over-come the limitations these roots have imposed. But changing such ingrained thoughts is a slow and painful process that many people never even *understand*, much less begin to accomplish. The older the individual, the less likely significant change will ever occur without outside help, such as provided in this book.

It's much easier to lay the foundation for a vigorous and healthy self-image and self-esteem during childhood than to heal a badly wounded and debilitated psyche in adult-hood. How we lay this essential groundwork will be the primary focus in later parts of this book. For now, however, we need to clearly understand the debilitating behaviors that are so characteristic of people with low self-image and self-esteem.

Among the worst of these problems are fear, despair, feelings of hopelessness, the use of victim language and destructive criticism, and constantly letting negative emotions rule our lives.

Before we examine these and some related maladies in more detail, let me pause a moment and ask you to do some homework. If you have never been to a group "recovery" meeting for alcoholics (e.g., Alcoholics Anonymous) or other substance abusers, please arrange to go to one. (Alternatively, try to find a local class or seminar on self-esteem.) There are literally thousands of such groups nationwide and dozens in every large city. You can locate them through your local church, newspaper, or telephone yellow pages. What you commonly find is a casual, warm atmosphere where you are readily accepted without question. All you need to do is go, sit, and listen.

Are you wondering why I would ask you to do this if you or someone close to you doesn't *have* a substance abuse problem? Because nowhere else will you find a gathering of individuals with such universally low and debilitating self-image and self-esteem.

> ### *It's not what you are that holds you back; it's what you think you are not.*

You can definitely *learn* from their stories. You will likely see examples, as I have, of people who are totally out-of-touch with the reality of their own self-image. Recently, I listened as one 25-year-old woman, a physically beautiful person in all respects, repeated *her* vision of herself as ugly and unappealing in every aspect—from her legs all the way up to her smile.

You can learn how seemingly innocent mistakes made by the parents of these individuals have profoundly affected their self-image and self-esteem for years or even decades. You can observe firsthand how crippling the malady of low self-image and self-esteem can be in an individual's quest for success in life.

You may notice several important and recurring themes. For example, you will see that fear, despair, and hopelessness are among the more common traits of those with low self-image and self-esteem.

You may also observe that when such traits work their way into people's lives, their tendency is to let each setback, disappointment, roadblock, and heartbreak bring them down. They want to cry out, "Why me?" They rarely view the disturbing event from a healthier perspective—"What can I learn from this?" or "What logical, practical solution can I devise for this problem?"

Observing a group where the preponderance of individuals have low self-image and self-esteem may also enable you to better understand how a condition of **homeostasis** commonly develops. When people always want to hang on to the status quo, to remain firmly on the beaten path, they have reached homeostasis. It's a stout refusal (and fear) to change, evolve, or grow as a person. Individuals become rigid, inflexible, and dogmatic and try to keep everything, including reference groups and friends, just the same. Such a gradual hardening of the attitude has also been called **cyclosclorosis.**

As homeostasis and cyclosclorosis tighten their grip on people, they often overreact to even small setbacks and let them produce emotional disability. This tendency to read the worst into even the most trivial setback is cited by some psychotherapists as the key to a wide range of emotional turmoil, from depression to phobias, anxieties, and even panic attacks.

"When people continue to exaggerate the importance of their failures, it sets up a downward spiral of disappointment that can end up in depression," says Richard Wenzlaff, a psychologist at the University of Texas in San Antonio.

"When a student gets a **C** when he expects a **B** or **A**, and then inflates the significance of that information, he can initiate a self-defeating chain of thought: I'm going to do *poorly* in this class; I'm just not a *good* student; I'll *flunk* out of college; and finally, I'm a *failure* in life," says Wenzlaff.

In earlier studies led by Martin Seligman of the University of Pennsylvania, researchers found that the ability to take setbacks in stride was a fundamental key to success in a wide range of endeavors, from sales—where rejection is commonplace—to politics.

When dealing with setbacks in an irrational manner becomes the norm, we begin to feel that we have little or no control over our lives. When we feel out of control, we hesitate even more to move forward or away from the beaten path. We are less likely to take the necessary risks that allow us to achieve goals that lead to success.

Try the quiz below to get a picture of your feelings about control and your propensity to take risks. For each numbered statement, quickly choose either part **a** or part **b** to go with this statement:

I am more inclined to believe that...

1a. Promotions come through hard work and persistence.

1b. High pay is a matter of the right breaks.

2a. Marriage is a gamble.

2b. The number of divorces indicates that many people do not know how to make a marriage work.

3a. It's useless to try to change.

3b. If I'm right, I can usually convince others.

4a. I cannot really influence the way other people behave.

4b. People can be led if one knows how to deal with them.

5a. My efforts alone determine my grades; luck is not a factor.

5b. At times, I feel like I have little influence over the grades I get.

6a. Certain people are almost impossible to please.

6b. Getting along with people is a learned skill that must be practiced.

7a. I alone will determine my fate.

7b. Much of what happens to me is by chance.

If you chose "a" for statements 1, 5, and 7, and "b" for statements 2, 3, 4, and 6, you feel in control of your life. The greater the number of your selections that deviated from these ideal choices, the less power or control you feel over *your own* life right now.

Fear, despair, and hopelessness generally set in as the amount of control you feel over your life diminishes. A number of other telltale signs emerge, too, as these indicators of low self-image and self-esteem begin to rule your life.

One of the surest signs of trouble is the use of what has become known as "victim language." Victim language centers around the use of these all-too-familiar phrases: **I can't** (do something); **I have to** (do something); **I wish** (I *could* do something); and **I'll try** (to do something).

The **I can't** and **I have to** statements are the most common form of victim language. Most of us either make, or hear others make, such statements on a daily basis. The examples are endless. Whether it's "I can't balance my checkbook" or "I can't get along her" or "I have to go," the underlying message is clear. We are identifying an area in our lives over which we *perceive* we have little control.

As our feelings of control diminish even further, we may revert to the even more dangerous and serious **I wish** language. Do phrases like "I wish I could get a better job" or "I wish I didn't have such a temper" sound familiar? What makes such talk so serious is that when we use the **I wish** preface, we're actually programming our subconscious minds to accept the situation as being hopeless. We're planning in advance for failure. We not only show that we lack control, but we're stating up front that we don't plan on seeking it!

The worst victim language of all, however, is the **I'll try** talk. "I'll try to stop drinking" or "I'll try to get along better with my coworkers" or "I'll try to make our marriage work" are the kind of statements we've all either made or heard from others. This kind of talk also shows that we *expect* to fail, so we're greasing the skids in advance. Our subconscious minds use such talk to prepare us for imminent *failure*.

Once we begin the use of victim language, our reliance on and use of negative emotions is never far behind.

The list of negative emotions is lengthy; over 50 have been identified in textbooks. What is so surprising is that *all* negative emotions are learned. We come into this world without *any* of them!

> ## *As ye think, so shall ye become.*

The most common negative emotions we are likely to display or see displayed around us are: worry, anxiety, fear, guilt, jealousy, and anger. But in fact, most, if not all, negative emotions eventually end up being displayed as the latter one—anger.

One of the most insidious negatives is destructive criticism. Destructive criticism is when we attempt to change someone's behavior, skills, or appearance to a desired outcome by stressing the undesirable outcome. Basically, it's when we try to chop a person down as a means of building them up.

We're applying destructive criticism when we use a statement like "You're not much good at baseball" instead of something more positive such as "With some extra batting and catching practice you'll do just fine." It's saying "You're an obnoxious little brat" instead of "You'd feel much better about yourself if you treated other people better." It's when we say "You're ugly" instead of "You have a beautiful smile and eyes; you should show them off more."

The use of destructive criticism is a systematic destroyer of your self-image and self-esteem. Age is no barrier. However, the most severe and long-lasting effects occur when it is used on children, up to age 5 or 6.

Do you think people learn to do the action better when they are repeatedly exposed to destructive criticism? No, they simply learn to *avoid* the action altogether. Our sub-conscious minds learn the lesson well: If I don't take any risks in this area, I won't have to suffer any more pain.

Destructive criticism is particularly damaging to children because their minds are so inexperienced and vulnerable. Children can't yet separate truth from fiction. So they *accept* all of the destructive criticism as reality, and they store it—sometimes forever—in their subconscious minds. That's why destructive criticism, plus lack of love (or *conditional love*), have terrible, long-lasting effects on their developing personalities.

> ### *Fear of criticism is the kiss of death in the courtship of achievement.*

The child or adult who is the repeated victim of destructive criticism and its attendant negative emotions is like a car with the emergency brake permanently applied. That car can still be driven forward but only very slowly. And each time it moves forward, the cost of doing so, in terms of wear and tear on all the parts, is tremendous.

Destructive criticism and the other factors which act to systematically lower people's self-image and self-esteem often lead to the lowest form of destructive criticism: race hatred.

Take, for example, a young man named Tom Martinez. In his early 20s, unemployed, with a wife and small baby, he saw David Duke, then Grand Wizard of the Knights of the KKK, on TV.

Martinez recalls thinking, "Damn, this guy is right! Who

is this guy?" From that point on he was hooked. He lived and breathed organized racism through participation in Duke's Klan, neo-Nazi groups, and eventually the Order, an Aryan Nations offshoot. His colleagues were murderers and robbers who wanted to overthrow the U.S. government and establish their own "homeland."

Martinez was eventually arrested, and to lessen his sentence, he "rolled over" and started working for the FBI and Secret Service. His part in helping bring down members of the Order was the beginning of his long journey back to self-respect. Today, in his mid-30s, he has become a crusader against the very hate he once professed. He crisscrosses the country speaking to students and community groups about the dangers of the race-hate organizations.

It has taken Martinez many years, but he now understands the factors that led him early on into the world of race hatred. Those factors were poverty, anger, the need to find a scapegoat, and above all, low self-image and self-esteem. He now knows that hate groups are like all cults. They make you feel important and wanted. They convince you that the rest of the world is wrong. But he now admits "no one is born a racist."

Racism also played a major role in the life of Robert Henry Nicolaus, who, as discussed earlier, murdered his three children and wife. Nicolaus was a stout racist and admirer of Hitler by his mid-20s. He even wanted his wife and children to wear swastika arm bands.

Another ugly hate example has appeared much more recently. In November 1993, police in Sacramento, California, arrested an 18-year-old high school student named Richard Campos as a prime suspect in five racially-motivated fire bombings. The fire bombings, which began in July and received nationwide news coverage, had terrorized Sacramento's minority communities.

Gradually, Campos' hate and feelings of white race supremacy are being revealed. His classmates and teachers say he is a model of self-destructive, violent behavior.

"He's a guy that's full of hate," said one fellow student. "He'd kill cats and put them on people's doorsteps, or crank call people and record them. I was scared of him."

He once etched an anarchist symbol and "Death to the Handicapped" onto one of his school binders. Other attention-getting exploits included butting his head against poles, lockers, and concrete walls or crumbling glass in his hands until they bled or putting glue in his hair. When he wasn't hurting himself, he was provoking, bullying, and intimidating others, male and female. He reportedly once threw a coffee can full of excrement at a female classmate.

What can we surmise about how Campos feels about himself? His bizarre behavior and treatment of others is likely a reflection of his own poor self-image and self-esteem. And his hostile actions invite criticism and rejection, which in turn further deflate his feelings of self-worth.

Another common malady of people such as Campos, who are lacking in or have greatly impaired self-image and self-esteem, is that they exhibit a poor attitude and lack of ethics in doing their jobs. They see things backwards. They tend to forget that it was they who asked for the job. They tend to feel that their employer owes them something, rather than the other way around. They're also more apt to steal from or cheat their employer to make up for low pay or other undesirable conditions. And people with low self-image and self-esteem are more likely to quit their jobs over trivial or unimportant matters that would be of little consequence to someone with healthy self-esteem.

It has also been shown that the worker with low self-esteem is usually more poorly dressed and often has a more disorganized work space than his healthier counterpart.

PART THREE:

The Tools and Skills

CHAPTER 7

Basic Guidelines

Highlights

✧ *Look close at hand for new opportunities and changes.*

✧ *Beware the emotional boomerang effect.*

✧ *Never blame yourself or feel guilty because of the way one of your children turned out.*

Through discussions of the maladies that limit us in the previous section, I'm sure that some of the techniques and methods for ensuring success are gradually emerging. Before we begin to build and expand upon these, we need to lay down a basic foundation of knowledge. This foundation is essential for better understanding and remembering the basic techniques and methods. Certain aspects of this foundation are probably already familiar to you, but in other parts we will likely break new ground.

Let's begin with a brief examination of three simple concepts or guidelines. Call them guidelines because, while they apply to most individuals, there are occasional exceptions.

Guideline #1:
Look Close At Hand For
New Opportunities And Changes.

Many of the best opportunities to advance our employment, better our relationships, improve our health, or improve other aspects of our lives can be found right around us at any given point in our lives.

What goes around comes around.

The problem is that many people put on blinders and fail to recognize obvious opportunities. The all-too-frequent tendency is to believe that we've got to "move on" or "get a fresh start" or "get away from it all" to have meaningful change.

Too often this kind of thinking equates with a wish to run away from the undesirable conditions or problems. If this is our motive, we fail to see the forest for the trees and miss key opportunities. We fail to see them because we don't want to.

Guideline #2:
Beware The Emotional Boomerang Effect.

The idea here is that each and every genuine emotion that we express to another individual comes back to us— with redoubled force! This concept applies to every emotion, negative or positive. Whether we express anger, destructive criticism, praise, or love to another, we can expect him or her to eventually reciprocate sometime with more of the same. In other words, what goes around *does* indeed come around.

Guideline #3:
Never Blame Yourself Or Feel Guilty Because Of The Way One Of Your Children Turned Out.

The natural tendency of all parents is to blame themselves. The list of possibilities is endless: "I should have spent more time with her" or "I wish I hadn't smoked while I was pregnant" or "We shouldn't have gotten divorced" or "I should have gotten a better job and been a better provider."

Blaming ourselves for our children's shortcomings serves no useful purpose because it can't *change* the reality of the way things are. We can't go back and undo or redo mistakes we made in the past. We can only affect the future.

A more positive approach is to learn to accept the reality of the situation. Understand that this is the way it is and that blaming and feeling guilty won't change the past. Counter the blame and guilt with this affirmation: "I did the best that I was capable of doing with the knowledge, abilities, and skills I had at the time."

> *The greatest understanding you can have is to understand that it's okay not to understand.*

An affirmation like this one facilitates letting go of the past and focusing on the future. It's the future that's most important. The future provides our chance to do better—to do everything we can to remedy the situation or problem using all our experience and knowledge, including the skills and techniques provided in this book.

There's also one more important point to remember: It's never too late to begin the first day of *the rest* of your life. We have the rest of our lives to make positive changes for the better.

CHAPTER 8

Basic Principles

Highlights

✧ *Use your subconscious mind as a partner.*

✧ *Fail your way to success.*

✧ *You have at least one area of excellence.*

✧ *You reap what you sow.*

Principle #1:
Use Your Subconscious Mind As A Partner.

Up to now, I've mentioned the subconscious mind, but it hasn't been formally defined. We need to take a few moments to talk about this extremely important concept.

The subconscious is that part of our mind that operates below or outside of the conscious mind. Other terms for the subconscious are robot, inner self, and inner person.

This inner person or robot holds all of our basic beliefs and values. And from these, the subconscious mind governs exactly who we are, including how we appear, act, think, react, feel, and talk. It's truly one of the most powerful and important aspects of the human psyche.

The subconscious mind is also where we have our perfect, all-encompassing memory—a memory of everything we've ever seen, felt, tasted, touched, and heard. This memory is perfect because it accepts and permanently stores everything without questioning its validity or accuracy.

Unfortunately, the subconscious mind works on the GIGO principle; this acronym, an offshoot of computer terminology, means that if we put garbage in (GI), we get garbage out (GO). The more good things we put in, the more good things we get out. And conversely, the more bad things the subconscious mind receives, the more bad output it directs us to produce at the conscious level. That's one of the key reasons parents must always strive to be good role models for their children. If children observe and hear mainly bad attributes, those attributes become the GI component of their subconscious minds that lead to GO.

Another key aspect of the subconscious mind is that it functions nonstop, 24 hours a day, no matter what we're consciously doing. It works when we're eating, talking, watching TV, and sleeping. In fact, the subconscious mind is even capable of solving our most pressing problems while we sleep. During sleep is also when it is more "programmable" with either good or bad input.

Our subconscious mind can be accessed directly by another person through hypnosis. And each of us, without the aid of hypnosis, continually accesses our subconscious mind—or more accurately, it *guides* us—in making hundreds, if not thousands of daily decisions and actions.

Another characteristic of the subconscious mind is that it always responds better to stimuli than to pressure. To illustrate, have you ever met someone whose name you know, but you just couldn't think of it? Have you ever lost your keys and frantically tried to remember where you left them? Have you ever taken a test and just couldn't recall an answer? Trying to *force* the answer out of the subconscious usually proves unproductive. What we generally need to do is relax, let the pressure subside, and then calmly and reassuringly tell ourselves that the answer *will* come up in a moment, or at a certain time in the future.

Here's one final key point about the subconscious mind: It is the starting point for all significant change. We change what we are by changing what goes into our mind.

As ye think, so shall ye become.

Principle #2:
Fail Your Way To Success.

Every road to success is marked with some failures. All highly successful people know this. They understand and accept that these inevitable failures happen for one specific purpose: to teach us what we need to climb the ladder and reach our goals.

One recent study examined the backgrounds of over 500 of the most successful people in the U.S. The majority made it to the top only one or two steps beyond their greatest failures. And every one of these success stories involved multiple failures along the way.

The most classic "failure to success" example of all time was Thomas Edison. He probably failed at more experiments, and lost more money doing so, than any inventor in modern history. Yet he was one of our greatest inventors, with over 1,000 U.S. patents that made him hundreds of millions of dollars.

It reportedly took Edison over 17,000 failed experiments to produce the techniques governing what is today's modern latex rubber industry. After 5,000 tries at developing the light bulb, someone said to him: "You've failed so many times, why not just give up?" Edison's reply was that he hadn't failed 5,000 times, but that he'd successfully identified 5,000 ways that wouldn't work, and he was thus 5,000 ways closer to the solution!

Consider another household name—Walt Disney. Few people realize that he went completely broke seven times and recovered from an emotional breakdown before his entertainment empire finally became a success.

Like Disney and Edison, we need to understand and embrace the principle that failing is an integral step on the ladder to success. This won't always be easy. Too many of us suffer from the malady called fear of failure, which keeps us from even *trying*. Specific ways to offset this malady are addressed later.

> ## *A big shot is just a little shot who kept shooting.*

Principle #3:
We Each Have At Least One Area Of Excellence.

Each of us develops a great many skills and abilities that are average or normal. In other words, the majority of us are average in most respects.

But it is just as true that each of us has been endowed with one or more inherent traits or abilities that are well above the norm which offer us the opportunity to achieve greatness, or at least excellence, in at least one area of our lives. This concept is consistent with the religious or philosophical belief that we were all put here for a purpose, to contribute something unique and specific to society and our planet. All highly successful people find their areas of excellence and channel their energies into fully developing and applying them.

> ***Working with the same material,
> one man may build a work of art,
> while the other
> whittles a pile of shavings.***

As adults, the rest of us have exactly the same challenge: to find and then develop our own area(s) of excellence. Sadly, far too few of us ever do so.

The maladies that keep us right where we are—in the same old ruts, in the same go-nowhere jobs, in the same abusive or "losing" relationships and behaviors—keep us from finding our areas of excellence. Over time, the failure to obtain excellence in *something* gradually drives down our self-esteem and self-image. Eventually, we end up with a negative attitude and see ourselves as only mediocre and below average. We know we've reached this point when we look into a mirror and can't say, "I *like* myself!"

Fortunately, it's never too late for any one of us to begin to identify and develop our inherent area(s) of excellence. The exercises in the Goals and Goal-Setting chapter of this book are designed to help you to do just that.

Principle #4:
We Reap What We Sow.

This principle, sometimes referred to as the **Law of Returns**, is pretty straightforward: We only reap or take something away as a result of having sown something in the past. And the more we put in, the more we get back.

The Law of Returns applies to every aspect of our lives. There's a song by the late Harry Chapin, called *Cats in the Cradle*, which exemplifies the concept clearly. It's a sad ballad about a father who finds that his son has "grown up just like me."

It's truly amazing how many people never understand the value of giving, sowing, and putting *in* something to get something *out* in return. Losers tend to think only in terms of what they can get out of a given situation or opportunity, rather than what they can *give* to get what they want.

CHAPTER 9

Other Related Laws And Concepts

Highlights

✧ *The more control you feel, the better you feel.*

✧ *If you lack control, you may just be "going with the flow."*

✧ *If you dislike an event, you can change it by changing the thought that causes it.*

✧ *You can suppress negative feelings by focusing on positive thoughts and things you desire.*

✧ *Whatever you truly believe, expect to happen, and concentrate on, your subconscious mind will pull towards you until it becomes reality.*

✧ *Mind work can't be forced like physical work. It needs to flow out. But mind work can be improved with practice.*

An earlier discussion illustrated how a feeling of lack of control over our lives is one of the major limits to self-improvement. Many psychologists go even further and assert that the degree of control we feel is a major factor in our overall feeling of well-being. I'll call this the **Central Well-Being Concept**.

When people feel little or no control over their lives, they may eventually just give up and start "going with the flow," wherever it may take them. When people reach such a condition, they may be described as living under **The Law of Accidents**.

The **Law of Cause and Effect** says that for every event that occurs there is a specific cause, even if we can't identify it. When we do not like the event that occurs, it is our responsibility to find the cause or causes and change them. Most often the causes are thoughts. Thus, by controlling our thoughts, we can control our lives much better.

The **Law of Substitutes** is based on the idea that we can only effectively focus on one major thought at a time. Therefore, if we substitute a positive idea or thought for a negative one, that positive idea will grow, blossom, and overwhelm the negative thought in our minds. We can be happier and eliminate negative emotions from our lives by focusing on what we desire instead of what we fear.

The **Law of Belief** states that whatever we truly believe, with emotion and feeling, becomes our reality. It doesn't matter if the belief is really true and based on reality—it will control our feelings and actions. Most of our self-limiting beliefs are not based on reality but misinformation, fed to us by parents and others and stored in our subconscious minds.

The **Law of Concentration** is similar. Whatever we dwell and concentrate on, we become. We become what we think about. The more we concentrate on it, the more we bring it into our lives.

The **Law of Subconscious Effort** says that the subconscious mind goes to work and brings into our reality whatever our conscious mind accepts and truly believes is possible.

The **Law of Attractions** is the concept that each person is a unique, one-of-a-kind being who attracts others who have certain distinct characteristics and beliefs. This can be either good or bad, depending upon whether those who harmonize with us are winners or losers.

The **Law of Mind Practice** states that we have to practice to become proficient at skills involving the mind, the same as we must for physical skills. For example, when we're not used to thinking positive thoughts, we have to practice over and over until they become a habit. Successful, positive-thinking people don't have to practice these mind skills; for them, such skills are already an ingrained habit.

The **Law of Mind Relaxation** is the idea that in mental or mind work, effort often defeats itself. We can't *force* mind work (i.e., *thinking* a new way) like we do physical work. It's often better to simply relax and confidently believe that the desired outcome will occur. When we're ready, the new thought process will automatically flow to us. Trying to force this flow often results in enormous stress and personal chaos.

The **Law of Expectations** says that whatever we expect to happen *will* become our self-propelled reality. It doesn't matter whether the expectation is based on reality or not.

This is a particularly powerful concept that has been the subject of substantial research. For example, in one recent study a group of teachers were told they had been picked as the best teachers in the school and that they were being assigned the school's brightest children for their classes. They were asked not to relate this secret to the children.

At the end of the year, the children the teachers had been told were the brightest led the entire school district in academic achievement and test scores. Only then were the teachers told the truth: The students assigned to them had been selected totally at random and were just an average subset of the school's population.

As ye think, so shall ye become.

This and hundreds of similar studies have demonstrated the power that expectations—whether based on true or false beliefs—can have on performance and achievement. As a result, many schools today boost achievement by using techniques to elevate expectations about the students.

CHAPTER 10

Risk-Taking And Accepting Failures

Highlights

✧ *Your ability to take risks and accept failures depends mostly on how you were treated as a child.*

✧ *Encouraging parental language teaches children to take risks and accept failures.*

✧ *Compare your child's improvements to his or her own past performances, not that of others.*

✧ *Encourage your child to try the widest range of activities possible without designating activities for boys and for girls.*

✧ *Teach your child safe boundaries and limits while encouraging exploration.*

✧ *Instill confidence in your child and encourage conversation about anything without fear of repercussion.*

What type of personality allowed Thomas Edison to fail at thousands and thousands of experiments, yet be driven to continue on until he achieved the successful outcomes he sought? Clearly he was a person for whom risk-taking and acceptance of failures had become a normal, nonthreatening, and even healthy aspect of life.

> *A well-adjusted person is one who makes the same mistake twice without getting nervous.*

What's the key to developing such a healthy viewpoint? It starts with how parents treat their children, especially during the first few years of life when the foundation of personality is being developed.

It's at this time that we want children to *learn* as much as possible and *do* as many things as possible, both physically and mentally. To help make this happen, we must continually encourage our children and help to expand their learning horizons.

The idea is to foster the maximum level of curiosity and risk-taking. (Note: Risk-taking, as used here and throughout the book, does *not* mean taking dangerous risks with your body or health.) Unfortunately, many parents do just the opposite and never realize it!

We need to recognize and avoid the use of *discouraging* language. Here's a sampling of what I mean:

"You can't do it; let me do it for you."

"You aren't old enough (or big enough) for that."

"Why can't you be more like your brother?"

"Be careful! You watch yourself!"

"You did it again, didn't you?"

"No! I've told you a thousand times!"
"No, that's not the way to do it."
"Here, let me do it for you."
"When are you going to become responsible?"
"Why can't you even clean your room?"

Do any of these phrases ring any bells with you? They should! At one time or another, probably each of us has used, or had used against us, such words of discouragement.

Breaking the habit of *dis*couraging language and developing positive, *en*couraging language isn't easy and can't be learned overnight. But with persistence, patience, and practice, we can all learn to do it.

When we first begin eliminating our discouraging behavior and replacing it with encouraging talk is when the most care and patience is needed. The new talk may come as a jolt to both the user and the receiver. One transitional approach can be to tell your child something like, "I know it's hard...I understand." Equally helpful are such affirmations as "I think you can handle it" or "Do you want to give it a *try*?"

As the new, *encouraging* talk becomes the norm, the range of opportunities for encouraging are almost limitless. Here are but a few specific examples:

"Wow, you're definitely improving. Look at the progress you've made."
"Gee, I like the way you did that."
"I have faith in you; I know you'll do fine."
"Boy, you worked hard on that; I like the way you tackle a problem."
"Maybe you can find another way to make it work."
"It looks like you enjoyed doing that."
"Thanks, you helped a lot."
"I appreciate what you did."
"I'm glad you enjoy learning."

Recognition of *improvement* should always be couched in terms of how the child (or adult) is performing with respect to himself or herself, *not* to others. "Great! You have two more Bs than on the last report card" is always better than "You're still not performing as well as your sister."

Parents also need to show liberal recognition for both what has been learned (mental tasks) and what has been done (physical tasks): "You have learned to count to ten" versus "You have put ten of your toys away." In addition, be careful to show trust, respect, and belief in your child; for example you might say, "Let me know which book *you decide* to read."

In encouraging your child to learn and do as much as possible, certain boundaries and limits must still be maintained. One is with regard to the child's safety. Obviously, special care must be taken to provide adequate protection from medicines, toxic household chemicals, fire, burns, electrical shock, and other potentially serious hazards within the child's environment.

> ***Measure yourself not by what you have accomplished but by what you should have accomplished with your ability.***

And in today's society it is doubly important that we ensure the child knows how to gauge the issue of who to trust. Most young children can't really grasp all the subtleties involved with determining who to trust and when. "In a preschooler's mind, someone who acts nice, is nice," explains Thomas Power, Associate Professor of Developmental Psychology at the University of Houston. "Preschoolers rarely think about motives or intentions; they go by what they see."

Teaching young children how to stay safe around other people takes patience, persistence, and sensitivity. What we want to do is *teach* them without frightening them. One key is to always keep our messages simple and avoid vague terms that the child may not yet fully comprehend.

Instead of saying, "Never get into a car with strangers," we can define with whom they *can* go—for example, mom, dad, and auntie. A similar approach can be used with other rules that might otherwise be too vague.

You can also educate your child against hazards through stories. Preschoolers especially love to conjure up stories, so encourage them to produce tales in which they have some brush with danger, but ultimately remain safe. You can easily initiate such interactions when giving your child a bath or when driving somewhere by playing the "what if" game. Ask questions such as "What would you do if we went to the store and suddenly you couldn't see daddy?" or "What would you do if *anybody* ever touched you down there?" The child's answers will help him or her to learn and you to gauge what still needs to be taught.

Raising young children who know how to stay safe is largely a game of instilling confidence in them, and the parent is the key player. Ultimately, you want to help your child learn to trust his or her own instincts enough to negotiate whatever situation comes up.

Achieving this ideal state necessitates that you keep your own emotions in check. Children must be made to feel that they can reveal anything that's bothering them without fear of parental repercussion.

Once children enter school, the encouraging talk should continue, so that they can continue to experience the widest possible range of mental and physical stimulation. Among other things, avoid teaching your child that there are "boy" things and "girl" things to do and participate in. Encourage your child to try *anything* that interests him or her, regardless of its normal gender base. If your child chooses an activity

that is a little "odd," give support for his or her not being
just like everyone else. Always encourage your child to display, use, and be proud of his or her own individual
uniqueness.

> *Every accomplishment, great or small,*
> *begins with the same decision:*
> *I'll try.*

Dr. Wayne W. Dyer, a noted motivational speaker and
psychologist, relates a story of how his own daughter
returned home from school one day in a distraught
condition. Wednesdays were "tumbling" day in gym class
at school. All the girls were supposed to wear shorts to school
under their dresses or skirts on Wednesdays. But on this
particular Wednesday, Dr. Dyer's daughter forgot to wear
her shorts and was summarily given two choices: either
tumble as she was, or go home. A warning letter was placed
in her school file, and this was what was really causing her
concern.

Dr. Dyer lovingly but firmly brushed aside his child's
concern and assured her that if she was to grow up to be
her own unique, free person with a full range of experiences,
she was going to eventually have several "ticklers" in her
school files.

Maximizing a child's experiences at school and fostering
uniqueness isn't always easy. Consider, for example, the way
sports are handled in most schools. We usually emphasize
selection of the best athletes because the only goal is winning
the game. As a result, only a handful of children end up
participating.

This isn't, however, the norm everywhere. Consider the
unique approach taken by one school in Plainfield, Indiana—

the Plainfield Community Middle School. Something called "widespread participation" has been adopted by the school, allowing more involvement of more children in more activities.

School Principal Jerry Goldsberry recalls, "We wanted to come up with a no-cut policy. How are students ever going to learn their strengths and weaknesses, likes and dislikes, unless they are given a chance to try?"

What this has meant in practice is that every child has an equal chance to feel like an important part of a team or activity. If a child wants to sing in the choir, he can; if a child wants to be on the swim team, run track, or be a cheerleader, she can. The school found they could apply the wide-open policy to all but two sports—volleyball and basketball—where limited space necessitated teams of finite size.

> *Risks must be taken, because the greatest hazard in life is to risk nothing.*

Not surprisingly, Plainfield's students have come out in droves. And has the no-cut policy devastated the success of the school's teams? Not so. "Last year, we had eight championships," explains Geoff Bradley, a coach and teacher.

One girl at Plainfield summed up the feelings of the children about the program. "Next year, I'm going to high school," she said. "There, I know I won't make the cheerleading squad. I know there'll be lots of girls better than me. But at least I got to have the experience. And that's something I'll remember all my life."

CHAPTER 11

Goals And Goal-Setting

Highlights

✧ *Hundreds of studies have proven that goal-setting is a key element of success.*

✧ *Goals are also essential to our well-being.*

✧ *Relatively few people have clear goals, and even fewer write them down.*

✧ *Basic reasons we don't set goals are:*
  ✧ *we aren't taught how to do it;*
  ✧ *we're discouraged from pursuing our goals by people around us;*
  ✧ *we're held back by fear of failure.*

Welcome to one of the most exciting parts of this book! I say this wholeheartedly because you can gain so *much* power and potential for personal advancement by mastering the techniques of goal-setting. As a result, I want to spend a little more time here than in other sections of the book.

What I have to tell you about goals and goal-setting is

well-proven. There have been hundreds of studies that reach the same basic findings and conclusions. The consensus is that virtually all peak-performing, successful people are habitual goal-setters. Learning these techniques and principles for yourself, and teaching them to your child, assures you both of a big step up the ladder to success.

Goal-setting is the steering wheel for our lives. Imagine your automobile traveling down the road. Without a steering wheel, the vehicle goes either left or right, and eventually leaves the road. Your surroundings are the only determinant of where you go.

> ## *We may never see the targets people aim at; we may only see the targets they hit.*

The same thing happens with our lives. Without goals, we'll eventually end up in a proverbial ditch, or wherever else our surroundings lead us.

Having no goals is akin to taking one of the world's best pistol shooters, blindfolding him, spinning him around, then asking him to strike the targets. Can he do it? Of course not! It's impossible. Even the most skilled person becomes useless at the mastered task.

How can you expect to hit a target you cannot see? This is exactly the situation into which the person without goals is thrust. We become like the car without a steering wheel, a ship without a rudder, or the shooter wearing a blindfold.

Goals are the essential "targets" of all successful people. They are also the universal guiding force that has saved countless people placed under the most extreme hardships.

Many prisoners of war and hostages of terrorists, for example, have recounted how their goals—often related to wanting to see a loved one again—pulled them through their ordeals relatively intact mentally and spiritually.

Consider the almost unbelievable saga of Terry Anderson, the American held captive in Lebanon for almost 7 years— 2,455 days, to be exact. Anderson described the agony of a life in chains and blindfolds. He was placed in a prison for the innocent with a sentence of unknown length where the empty days evolved slowly into weeks, months, and years. His food was thrown on the floor. This 7-year saga played out in a small, daylightless cell where rigid rules, such as being allowed to go to the bathroom only once each day, were enforced by brutal guards.

What brought him through those 7 years of hell with his mind and spirit still relatively healthy and intact? A goal— to see his daughter Sulome who was born after his capture— was one major force. His captors almost certainly under-estimated the power of the single, small photograph of her Anderson was allowed to have in his possession.

> *Hope sees the invisible,*
> *feels the intangible,*
> *and achieves the impossible.*

An equally uplifting story is recounted by Colonel Charles Scott. He was one of the 52 American hostages seized by terrorists at the U.S. Embassy in Iran in 1979. He endured 444 days of horrific confinement. He has scars on his feet from being beaten with a steel rod, his left shoulder was broken, and his captors knocked out most of his teeth over the long months. Much of the time he was not only alone in a small cell but kept chained and blindfolded as well.

Scott attributes his survival to his determining, the very afternoon of his capture, that he would set goals and objectives before the physical abuse he knew he'd have to endure actually began. Scott relates, "I survived because I had goals."

Scott's and Anderson's stories are far from unique. Dozens of American prisoners held in the north during the Vietnam War recount similar use of goals to not only survive but to keep their minds and spirits relatively intact and thriving.

> ## *It's better to have a hen tomorrow than an egg today.*

An inevitable question must logically now arise. If goals are not only essential to our success in life but often critical as well to our actual *survival*, why is it that so few people have them? Right now, probably less than 5 percent of the population has clear goals, and 1 percent of us may have actually written them down.

Most of the blame falls within three key areas. First, we're never taught about the importance of goals and goal-setting. How much of this kind of instruction did you get in school? How much are your children getting today? Did your parents ever teach you about goals? Sadly, the average person's answer to each of these questions is, "Little to none."

Second, even for the fortunate few of us who were actually educated on the subject, or who happened onto some of the key principles on our own, we may have lacked support from those around us. This in turn may have kept us from fully utilizing goal-setting techniques. Many of us heard these all too familiar remarks: "You can't" or "You shouldn't" or "Don't even try—it'll never work." Without the needed encouragement, we usually avoid even trying to use goal-setting methods.

The third and sometimes most important reason the majority of us don't set and pursue goals is our fear of failure. It may not be the negative thoughts of others that influence us the most. Those negative thoughts are ingrained in *our own* subconscious mind by now. The negative thoughts coming *from within* us, due to our own low self-image and self-esteem, are now controlling factors.

Fear of failure often holds us back more than any other single factor. Many of us never learn, or learn only relatively late in life, that failure is an integral part of the road to success. Failures must therefore be accepted and should never be feared. I want to emphasize this again, because it is truly one of the most important principles we must master to achieve success.

Allowing fear of failure to keep us from setting goals is most prevalent when we have low self-image and self-esteem. These debilitating traits can be seen almost universally in children (and adult children) of alcoholics, drug addicts, and physically and sexually abusive parents. (If you haven't followed through on my previous suggestion, I urge you again to attend at least one meeting of a substance abuse recovery group, so you can see and learn firsthand about this important phenomenon.)

Our goals are our targets, our points of completion. Goals reflect our basic wants, desires, and dreams. They may involve anything of our choosing, from aspects of our lifestyle to job, family, or our environment.

Learning to apply the concepts of goal-setting is vitally important, because the process is so effective. This effectiveness derives from the involvement of the subconscious mind. Once a goal becomes the designated target and is fully committed to, our subconscious mind goes to work immediately, driving us unerringly towards the target and the goal's achievement. Whenever we're faced with decisions or judgments, our subconscious mind, having programmed the goal, ensures that we automatically make choices which facilitate goal acquisition. The process moves us steadily upward.

Consider my own case in point. For years, since 1979, I'm embarrassed to admit, I fiddled sporadically and often half-heartedly with the idea of writing this book. I collected bits of literature here and there. I made a few notes and outlines. Occasionally, I even scratched out a paragraph or two.

But only when the book became a part of my own major life goals did things begin to really click. It was at this point that I felt unstoppable and irresistibly drawn towards the goal. At this point, I could make decisions more quickly and easily. As a result, the whole project, which includes self-publishing and both mail-order and bookstore promotion of the book, fell into place in 6 months of mostly weekend work. This occurred after more than 10 years of intermittent work during which no significant progress was made.

I believe that anyone can get into the same automatic, unstoppable, goal-attainment mode that I used to produce this book. Simply elevate what has been your dream to the status of a true goal. Then program the goal for automatic success, following the procedures below. Your sense of satisfaction and feeling of well-being will be unbelievable!

Remember, too, that in addition to being the pathway to your dreams, goal-setting and achievement may be beneficial to your overall health. Conversely, goal deprivation may be just as debilitating as dream deprivation is while we are sleeping.

Numerous studies of sleep/dream relationships confirm that very serious and debilitating effects occur if we are deprived of dreams (usually done experimentally by awakening the individual just as dreaming starts). We become irritable, irrational, and quick to anger. We may even develop physical ailments. Such effects occur even when we are allowed our normal amount of sleep, if we are prevented from dreaming. As soon as we're allowed to dream at will, without disturbances, the negative effects quickly subside.

Having established the critical importance of goals to individual success (and perhaps health), let's now turn to two of the more nuts-n-bolts questions: 1) How do we find and focus in on our goals? and 2) How do we program them for success?

Focusing In: The Start.
Highlights

♦ *Get your goal-setting engine going by answering seven questions.*

♦ *Then go back and reconsider any conflicting answers.*

Getting your goals into focus requires some written work. I encourage every reader to do the following exercise. You'll need at least two regular-sized sheets of paper (or use some of the blank pages provided at the end of this book) and something to write with. If the topic is new to you, it is essential that you do it fully. However, even the experienced goal-setter can find considerable value in working through these questions.

From your answers to seven important questions, you can begin to form a complete set of meaningful, personalized goals.

These questions are more appropriate and meaningful for adults and teenagers than for children. However, you may find that even a child in grade school can work effectively and meaningfully through at least some of them.

Use your judgment as to applicability. If your child can't meaningfully answer a question, don't worry. The important thing is that *you* learn about and understand the process, so you can help teach it to him or her later. You will likely need to read this part of the book more than once to grasp all its nuances.

Now, let's begin. Where time limits are given, try to stick to them. First, write down your answers to this key question as quickly as possible (no more than 2 minutes): **1) What four things do I value most in life, right now?** Your answers will form a foundation upon which you can base long-term goals.

Next, working even more quickly—in 30 seconds or less if you can—answer this question: **2) Right now, what are the two most important goals in my life?** This is a quick-list method that will help you assess where you are at in the process. The goals will be the most important and the most accurate for this particular point in time if you list them spontaneously. A lack of at least two complete answers may underscore your need to work carefully and fully through this section of the book.

Now, taking more time if you need to, write answers to the third question: **3) What would I do if I found out tomorrow that a distant relative had died, leaving me two million dollars, tax free?** The important thing to note about this question is that virtually anything you write down is within the realm of possibility. Anything on this list can be attained; all that's needed is to want it badly enough!

The fourth question may require some deeper thought: **4) What would I do for the next 9 months if I learned today that's how long I have to live?** Think carefully about this, then write your answers down. Consider what you'd do and what changes you'd make in your life. Think about who you'd want to see or where you'd want to go. Take time to carefully think about your answers; they may direct you to where your true values lie. They may help you to begin to see what is *really* most important to you.

Question five should be easier: **5) What have I always wanted to do but been afraid to try?** The more you can write here, the more likely your life has been, until now, ruled by your conditioned responses to fear of failure. If this is true, focus on elevating your self-image and self-esteem and destroying this negative habit. Follow the specific techniques spelled out in the following pages to accomplish this.

If you have trouble writing down *any* answers here, congratulations are in order! You may be someone already high up the ladder to success. You can spend your time focusing on the newer or more subtle issues and techniques that you may not have had previous exposure to.

Question six is another one that may require some in-depth thinking: **6) What things do I do now in my life that give me the greatest enjoyment, satisfaction, and feelings of self-worth?** The answers you give here are essential in identifying where your true areas of excellence lie. If these answers are considerably different than those for the earlier questions, you may have to resolve conflicts between what you *think* you want and what you are adapted to achieve most easily and readily.

Now, write down your answer to the seventh and final question: **7) If I were granted any one wish, what would it be?** Each of us has played this one in our minds at some point, usually as children. Try to think this time around as if it is an absolute certainty that you will get your wish. This will help reveal what your one great dream in life is. As shown later, if you can dream it, write it down on paper, think it, visualize it, and believe it, you can have it!

Now take a few minutes to go back and look over your answers.

Are there any surprises? Were you forced to dig hard to answer any of the questions, or did the answers flow easily? Do any of the answers seem in conflict? If there are conflicts, you will need to think about your responses again, with particular attention to questions 6, 1, and 4, in that order; this extra effort can help reveal your true feelings.

Before you can use this new information to develop your first set of goals—or refine an existing list if you're already a habitual goal-setter—let's examine a few more principles and guidelines specific to the goal-setting process. Without this added information, the exercise just completed may prove enlightening but won't be of much practical use.

Principles And Guidelines.
Highlights

- ✧ *Goals must always be self-directed. This is because the starting point for any goal is desire, and it's impossible to feel another person's desire.*

- ✧ *Goals should utilize your area(s) of excellence. Choosing a goal outside your area(s) of excellence can be difficult because your mind may not accept the goal as realistic.*

- ✧ *Goals should not be too difficult, but they should make you stretch to your full potential.*

- ✧ *You may need to break large goals down into smaller increments.*

- ✧ *Goals must be well-defined, using as much descriptive detail as possible, and given a clear timetable.*

- ✧ *The more benefits and advantages to a goal's achievement that you can think of and write down, the more powerfully you will be drawn to it.*

- ✧ *"Give-up" goals can be shared with most other people; "go-up" goals should only be shared with those you know will support you.*

If you remember nothing else from your first reading of this important section, remember this: *A person's goals must be self-directed.* In other words, you cannot have a goal for someone else, especially a goal that involves major changes to another person's life. You can only achieve goals directed to yourself.

This limitation arises because the starting point of any goal is *desire*. And while you can help someone else gain desire, you can neither force it upon them nor have their desire for them. A goal to have someone else stop smoking, drinking, or abusing drugs is clearly inappropriate. Similarly, getting someone you know to lose 50 pounds cannot effectively be brought to fruition through any goal-setting you do. Individual goals must always be your own, fostered by your own wants and desires.

Another key goal-setting principle is to focus first within your own area of excellence. As discussed earlier, each of us has particular areas in which we excel and from which we derive our maximum pleasure, fulfillment, and feeling of self-worth. It's our responsibility to find these areas and put them to work in pursuit of our goals. When we do this, we discover that desire, which is also essential, is already there waiting to be deployed.

> *Give me a clerk at Burger King with dreams, and I'll give you a person who'll make history; give me a person without dreams, and I'll give you a clerk at Burger King.*

Attempts to pursue goals outside of our area(s) of excellence can be difficult and even counterproductive. One problem is that deep in our minds we may not see a goal as realistic. For example, if we set out to become a science fiction writer of the caliber of Ray Bradbury, but we've never really enjoyed English and writing, that goal may not be believable. The same thing applies if we decide to become a renowned woodcarver but are lacking in artistic talent. When our subconscious doesn't view a goal as realistic, there's usually little chance that the burning *desire*, another essential ingredient, is going to be present.

Don't overdo this principle, however. It applies to the adult or teenage reader. There's much less need for younger children to concentrate their goals in their area(s) of excellence. For one thing, they may not yet have displayed any such areas. Second, it's important to encourage children to experiment and try out a wide range of activities and experiences. Basically, they need to become avid, albeit managed, risk-takers. Soon enough, their areas of excellence will begin to emerge and can then be applied in the pursuit of goals.

Once we focus on an area of excellence, or where such excellence can reasonably be developed, we can initially set small, realistic goals. This ensures success. Each goal that we attain brings feelings of well-being which in turn generate the necessary enthusiasm and confidence to move on to the next goal. We gradually become unstoppable, just like a chain reaction. This is one of the surest ways to wipe out old behaviors, especially those governed by the fear of failure.

Inch by inch, anything's a cinch.

Realistic and believable goals are absolutely essential, however, because our subconscious minds are not easily fooled. And it is the subconscious mind that will ultimately do much of the work for us, as it automatically guides us to the target. If the subconscious mind does not believe the goal is within our capabilities, this automatic guidance system shuts down, and unfortunately, there is no backup system.

On the other hand, our goals must not be too easy to achieve. This won't be a problem initially. But, as we become more proficient at defining targets and consistently hitting them, we need to be sure to set subsequent targets farther and farther back. The idea is to learn to stretch to our full potential in achieving each new goal.

This simple example should illustrate some of the points I've just made. Let's say that you presently earn $25,000 a year and have decided to substantially increase your income. Setting an income goal of $1,000,000 or even $200,000 next year might not be realistic and believable. And a goal of $27,000 next year might not involve much stretching. However, a step-by-step series of goals to earn $30,000, $50,000, and $100,000 in 1, 3, and 5 years, respectively, is plausible. Such a series of goals will also progressively stretch you farther and farther to your full potential. Your subconscious mind should readily accept this plan and go to work guiding you through this series of targets.

It is often better to set a series of goals than to try for one large, and possibly unrealistic, goal all at once.

The process is analogous to the approach of pole-vaulters or high-jumpers. Do they set the bar at the world record level on their first jump? No! They begin with a jump they know they can achieve. This polishes form and builds confidence for the next jump, then the next, and the next.

These athletes also have very specific, well-defined goals, for example, 6 feet 11 inches or 15 feet 10 inches. The goals we set must likewise be well-defined. In fact, this is one principle to be taken to the extreme. Always define your goal with the greatest possible detail. This aspect of goal programming cannot be overdone.

It isn't enough, for example, to simply state that your goal is a new car or a new house. You need to describe every specific feature of that new car or house. For a car, it may be the exact make, model, color, and all optional features that you desire. A new house might best be defined in terms of its type or method of construction, size, location, age, the exact number and kind of rooms, and all its special features.

> ## *Beware of the man who won't be bothered with details.*

The more details you use to describe your goal, the easier and more effectively you can visualize it in your mind's eye. And just as it is for world-class athletes, the ability to effectively visualize your goals as already achieved is critically important. In fact, there's a growing body of evidence which says that our ability to *see* the completed goal beforehand may be every bit as important as the development of the physical and mental skills needed to reach it.

A key aspect of detailing that must not be overlooked is the timetable. Exactly when do you plan to reach a particular goal? You must define the date or time precisely. If the goal is large or otherwise formidable-appearing, however, always break it down into smaller components with their own milestone dates or times.

By breaking a big project into smaller components, we get pumped up each time a component is completed, readying us to tackle the next component and its due date. This makes us feel like winners and more in control of our lives. Those feelings in turn help guarantee the entire goal's attainment.

Another factor that helps guarantee goal attainment is to fully assess *why* you want it. In fact, you need to try to think of *all* the possible benefits and advantages that you can derive.

Benefits and advantages should always be thought of and stated as *positives* rather than *negatives.* Something like "I want to stop smoking so I'll live longer, feel better, have a better quality of life, and be able to watch my sons grow up" is better than "I want to stop smoking so I won't die of lung cancer or heart disease."

Write out on paper all the benefits and advantages for attaining your goal; include as much specific detail as possible. The more detailed the reasons you generate, the more powerfully your subconscious mind will draw you towards the goal. You will likely find that 3 or 4 reasons provide *some* impetus, 10 or 15 provide *substantial* motivation, and detailing 20 or more reasons for attaining a goal will make you unstoppable in the pursuit of it—just like an arrow headed for a target.

Take care to mix the types of goals you want to achieve. Research shows that the most success comes through the pursuit of a variety of kinds of goals at one time, for example, one each in such areas as family, financial, spiritual, business, and professional. This approach is more effective than the single-minded pursuit of one goal or the pursuit of goals in just one area, such as financial.

In developing a mix of goals, watch out for disharmony and contradictions. For instance, you might not be able to climb in the mountains, ski every day, and also live in the desert. Nor is it likely that you could be a beach bum at the same time you are a highly successful business or professional person. Remember, too, that your overall package of goals must be congruent and in sync with your basic, fundamental values.

Generally, your goals need not be congruent with other people's values or goals. But what about *sharing* goals with other people?

Whether or not we share our goals with others usually depends on who the others are and what type of goal is involved. "Give-up" goals, in which we're giving up something like cigarettes, alcohol, drugs, or fat, should be readily and freely shared with anyone who'll listen. This puts us on the spot and boosts our chances for success. You'll rarely find a naysayer who wants to attack you for having this type of goal. In fact, most people with whom you share give-up goals will support you fully.

On the other hand, we must be more careful about sharing our "go-up" goals. Go-up goals involve getting more—power, money, possessions, respect, prestige, or whatever. These should only be shared with those who we know will support us in reaching them. Avoid the potential naysayers and negative people who would discourage rather that encourage you.

Step-By-Step Approach.
Highlights

* *You can program any goal for success, using this systematic nine-step approach.*

* *In the first six steps, you describe the goal in writing, along with related details.*

* *Consolidate the information into a complete plan as Step 7.*

* *Visualize repeatedly in your mind's eye the completed goal; make the visualizations as detailed and emotion-filled as possible. This is Step 8.*

* *Step 9 calls for keeping a positive attitude, vowing to never give up, and updating your goal plan as needed.*

* *These nine steps make you as unstoppable as a cruise missile headed for the target.*

You're now ready for a systematic, step-by-step approach to program your goals for success. You may see variations of this approach elsewhere, but these nine steps are the key elements, those most supported by exhaustive research.

If you're not already a habitual goal-setter, why not take the plunge right now? Why not set your very first goal—to actually work completely through this nine-step process in all of its detail—using one or more of *your own* goals! You're sure to learn and remember more than if you simply read this part.

> ***The elevator to success is permanently out of order; you're going to have to take the stairs—one step at a time.***

To ready yourself, go back and reread your answers to the seven-question quiz from Focusing In: The Start. Also, if you need it, refresh your memory on the just-completed Principles and Guidelines by reviewing the highlights at the beginning of the section.

Here are the nine steps:

Step 1. **Write down the goal.**

Remember to do this with all the specificity and detail that you can. Make it *your* goal, and something that *you* intensely desire. Make it realistic and believable. But be sure that it'll make you stretch. It should be neither too easy nor too hard. A good rule of thumb is that you should feel there's about a 50:50 chance for achievement. This should provide a happy medium between being believable and making you stretch.

Writing down the goal is the first step in the process for good reason; it's the most important step. Until you put the goal into writing, which starts the essential programming of your subconscious mind, you don't really have a goal, only a wish or a dream.

Step 2. Write down how you'll benefit by achieving this goal.

Remember that the key here is to be specific and go for sheer volume. Write down every imaginable advantage and benefit that you can. It may be helpful to arrange your answers in two columns labeled "Major" and "Minor" or use other categories of your choosing, such as "Family" or "Financial."

> *You have to have a dream if you're going to make a dream come true.*

Step 3. Write down the timetable.

Indicate exactly when you will complete the goal. Don't forget that big tasks or challenges may need to be subdivided, depending upon your level of experience with the goal-setting process. Remember that achieving sub-tasks has the benefit of spurring you on. So don't hesitate to develop a series of intermediate goals with their own deadlines within the timetable for completion of the main goal.

Step 4. Write down what you perceive to be the obstacles in your path.

There are always obstacles, believe it! If there weren't any, you wouldn't be dealing with a goal—it would simply be an *activity*.

This step has a very important purpose. Before you give systematic consideration to obstacles, they may seem totally overwhelming. That's one reason the goal hasn't *already* been achieved! But when you reduce the obstacles to writing, they invariably shrink in importance.

What you'll usually find is that only one or two of the obstacles have any real significance; the others become inconsequential and can be easily dealt with when written down and analyzed on paper.

Step 5. Write down the additional knowledge, tools, equipment, or skills you need.

This step is self-explanatory but may require some careful thought. At least some new knowledge is usually required. You need to identify whether this will come from resource people, books, on-the-job training, formal schooling, or other places.

Step 6. Write down the people, groups, and organizations with which you'll need to interact.

You *will* need things from others. It may be knowledge, financial assistance, training, or just simple cooperation. As you identify those you will need to interact with, think about what you can *give* in return for what you *get* from them. All successful men and women do this. Unsuccessful people usually do it in reverse; they think *only* about what they can get out of every situation.

Step 7. Develop a written, detailed plan.

If you want a new house built on a lot you own and approach a contractor, the first thing he says is, "Where's the plan?" By the same token, you need a detailed plan for each specific goal you pursue.

This written plan becomes the road map that will guide you directly to the goal. But don't worry, because the plan's already nearly completed. All you need do now is to appropriately combine the results of steps 3 through 6, dealing with the timetable, the obstacles, the new skills needed, and the people/groups with which you need to interact. Then just fill in the gaps and answer the obvious questions that should be readily apparent.

For example, how will you deal with the obstacles? Where and how will you get the new things you need? And, don't forget to identify what you can give the individuals and groups you need to work with in return for what you *need* from them.

Depending upon the goal, a final aspect of the written plan may be an accurate assessment of the *present* status. If your goal, for example, is to lose 50 pounds in 10 months at a rate of 5 pounds per month, state your exact weight now. If your goal is a financial one, you need to clearly define your present financial situation.

Step 8. Visualize, Visualize, Visualize!

Now it's time to begin "printing" again and again in your mind "pictures" of having already *achieved* the goal. Do these visualizations frequently. This is an area where you can easily become complacent. Yet it's one of the most powerful tools you have, an activity where even minimal effort pays big dividends.

Several other authors of step-by-step approaches to goal-setting and goal achievement believe that this is one, if not *the* most, important step in the process. Research has shown that virtually all top achievers and successful people in every field make liberal use of visualization techniques.

To have your visualizations make a maximum impact on achieving your goal, however, be sure to make them *very detailed* and incorporate, as much as possible, scenes involving *emotions*. For the detail you need, simply refer to the description of the goal you wrote out in Step 1. Then develop your appropriate mental pictures.

Putting emotions into your visualizations may at first require some thought and practice. Here are three ideas you can adapt and build upon for your particular goal: 1) picture an individual you love or whose opinion and praise you value shaking your hand, hugging you, or otherwise extending their congratulations; 2) picture similar praise from a group connected with your goal; 3) if the goal involves an audience of some sort, visualize them clapping and cheering for you.

> ## *Imagination is often more important than knowledge.*

To generate other ideas, consider some of the key visualizations that worked for me in pursuing this book. To be specific, I visualized my garage stacked with rows of boxes containing the first printing of the book. From a course I'd taken about how to self-publish and market a book, I knew that the books would come from the printer in boxes of 48, with each box containing 6 packages of 8 books, and each package tightly secured in clear shrink-wrapped plastic. So that's exactly what I visualized. I played movies in my mind of myself stacking, handling, and tearing open those beautiful little shrink-wrapped bundles as I prepared to mail the books to purchasers.

Since my primary book sales approach is through mail orders, I also visualized myself in various scenes at the post office, opening my mail drawer to reveal stacks of envelopes, each containing an order and check for the book.

Here's how I injected emotions into my vizualizations. In one scene, an acquaintance at work whose opinion I valued highly, but whose close friendship had never been secured, was shaking my hand and congratulating me after reading his copy of the book. Another set of visualizations involved various family members proudly touting the book to their friends and coworkers. I also developed scenes involving our family coming much closer together, with more loving interactions and communications.

Step 9. Resolve to keep practicing, planning, and persevering.

Now that you've labored to develop the plan called for in Step 7, accept that it will never be perfect. It is a road map to success, a steering wheel, a rudder, a computer guidance system. The plan will initially aim you at the target. But the path to any true goal always contains unexpected detours and, of course, setbacks. Expect them and realize that they're perfectly normal.

It's important to view all setbacks and detours with a positive frame of mind. Remember that they are there solely to teach you valuable lessons, to hone your existing skills or teach you new ones. Accept setbacks as essential to climbing up the next rung on the ladder to success.

> *What you commit yourself to become determines what you are.*

Whenever setbacks and detours happen, get out the plan and modify it accordingly. Don't hesitate to change the timetable or other parts. If necessary, rewrite your solutions to obstacles. Add individuals or groups to the list of those you'll be interacting with. Don't be afraid to rethink the skills and tools you need.

In short, change whatever you have to in the plan whenever you need to. This is where the plan for goals *is* truly different from a plan for building a house or other discrete object.

If you keep the plan updated and thus realistic, your subconscious mind continues to accept and *believe* it, guide your actions, and ensure continued progress towards achieving the goal. This helps keep you from giving up when the going gets tough.

> *Within every setback or disadvantage, there is the seed of an equal but opposite advantage or benefit.*

That, too, is a key point; vow to never give up! Keep repeating to yourself that, with persistence, you *will* prevail. All winners, top achievers, and successful people think this way.

One of these wise people summed it up this way: "All that is really required to have anything in life that you want is to do two things. First, determine exactly *what* it is that you really want. And second, simply resolve that you *will* pay whatever the price necessary to get it."

That kind of resolve is all that remains to be done once you have planned and programmed your goal for success, using the nine-step process we've just gone through. You then become unstoppable on your way to the target.

> *Luck is good planning, carefully executed.*

CHAPTER 12

The Winning Attitude

Highlights

✧ *Your positive, winning attitude is a prerequisite to success.*

✧ *This section focuses on adults, teens, and older adolescents.*

Check out the messages in the two boxes below. These are recent word-for-word classified advertisements from the "People Seeking People" sections of two local newspapers.

> *20-YEAR-OLD, lazy, fat, beer-guzzling slob. Heavily into Hogan's Heroes. Seeks Bob Crane admirer to watch TV with. Kind of a punk rocker, more of a loser-geek. Call XXX-XXXX.*

> *FAT CHICK wants boyfriend. No smoke, drug, drink. Eating OK! 1 kid-18, 1 dog, 3 cats. DWF sometimes witty, occasionally intelligent, always sarcastic. Have no life...call XXX Talk Category XXXX.*

Do these people sound like the kind of upward-moving individuals you'd like to associate with? Would you want your children around them? Unless you picture yourself like these two people in your thinking, your answer is a resounding "No." The overwhelmingly negative attitudes these people display tell their story: "If you're down and out, hang around me, and I'll help keep you there." This kind of thinking gives life to the old adage, "He's (or she's) a born loser."

But we need to remember that neither the people in these ads nor anyone else is "born a loser." It's everything that happens to us from birth onward that *conditions* us to either act like these losers or to exude the winning attitude.

This chapter focuses on the winning attitude—what it is, how we nurture and develop it, and how we rejuvenate it when it begins to slip away. And believe this: The vast majority of us will at times find our winning attitude regressing or slipping away!

When it happens, we need to know how to take corrective action. If I do my job well, this should be as simple as rereading this section of the book. That's why I've tried to keep this chapter brief, to the point, and filled with the most proven techniques. I know there's a good chance—in fact, an almost certainty—that you'll need to reread it occasionally.

This chapter is focused on the adult, or at least teenage, reader. A younger child will find the concepts too advanced. But that isn't a problem if you do a good job of *teaching* the other essential tools and skills, while *instilling* in your child a strong, healthy self-esteem and self-image.

Many of the points I'll raise in this section were indirectly stated or alluded to earlier, but they were scattered and fragmented. What I'll do now is bring them all together, add a few new key points, and then leave everything in one place where you can quickly and efficiently reference it whenever you need it.

Let's turn back to the "boozer" and "fat chick" ads. These two people obviously don't understand that a positive approach and attitude are always best. All high achievers exhibit such traits. Without a positive, winning attitude, we automatically limit ourselves to being mediocre at best.

The Attitude Regulator: How We Think.
Highlights

- ✧ *You can produce a winning attitude by the way you think.*
- ✧ *Deal with everyone in a friendly, positive manner.*
- ✧ *Add a positive affirmation to your wake-up routine.*
- ✧ *Greet telephone callers in a positive, upbeat tone.*
- ✧ *Avoid responding "tit for tat" by reframing the situation and "taking the blame."*
- ✧ *Replace victim language with positive statements.*
- ✧ *Praise yourself and others frequently.*
- ✧ *Avoid arguments by listening to what others have to say.*
- ✧ *Focus your thinking on your desires, not your fears.*

Where do such healthy attitudes begin? They are born from how we *think*! Authorities believe that up to 90 percent of the way we *feel* is actually determined by how we think. Positive thinking lets us *use* all the skills and abilities we already have. While it may not let us do everything, it does let us do everything better than we otherwise could have.

> ### *The fragrance of the rose lingers on the hand which casts it.*

Always *think* in a relaxed, friendly, and positive manner towards everyone you encounter. Starting each new day with positive thinking can really be effective in setting the trend for the whole day.

Start when the alarm clock goes off each morning. How should you react? You can scrunch down under the covers, begin to fret and worry, and maybe even get angry about the day that's facing you. You can try to hide under the covers for a few more precious moments of sleep. Or you can jump up and proclaim, "Wow! I feel great. What a day I'm going to have!"

The first time you try this, are you likely to *believe* it? Of course not! But that doesn't matter. This kind of positive affirmation will have several desired effects.

It immediately sets the tone for the day, priming you for a new, more positive frame of mind. It gives you an edge on controlling your life. And it can provide just the kind of "shocker" or precursor to change that you may need to start moving up.

Research has shown that this kind of quick, flamboyant gesture is just the ticket for starting really big changes in our lives. If we can force ourselves to make a positive morning affirmation for 21 to 28 days, an amazing thing occurs: We start to *really* believe it and feel it! This contrasts with the many years it has taken us to develop the bad habit of getting up in the morning "on the wrong side of the bed."

> ## *Be careful of your thoughts; they may become words at any moment.*

It's not hard to condition ourselves to get up each morning with a positive affirmation that gets us out the door in a good frame of mind. Our challenge for the rest of the day is to not let those we encounter bring us back down to *their* levels. If we encounter an aggressive driver on the way to work, we simply get out of their way. If we encounter a rude or obnoxious waitress at a restaurant, or if one of our coworkers resorts to these traits, we bite our tongue and hold our emotions in check.

If we respond instead with more "normal" behavior, based on "tit for tat" and the use of negative emotions to match negative emotions, we immediately lose control and let the other side bring us down to their level. Zig Ziglar, a great motivational speaker, has a good acronym for those of us who give in to our own negative emotions when confronted with the same. He calls us SNIOPs—susceptible to the negative influences of other people. The right thinking, however, can always prevent us from being a SNIOP.

Thinking in this manner isn't easy at first. But there's a very simple and powerful tool for ensuring that you don't lose *your* cool in an adverse encounter with someone else's negative emotions. Simply identify a sound, logical reason as to why the situation is really all *your* fault. You could say to yourself "I shouldn't have been in the left lane; that's why that driver tailgated me" or "It's my fault for eating there at their busiest time of day, when the waitresses are most stressed out" or "I should have realized that Mary would make a snide remark if I told her about my promotion."

When you accept the responsibility in this manner for any potentially adverse emotional situation, two important things occur. First, you gain another small increment of control over your own life, thereby giving yourself a boost. Second, you effectively deny the other side the chance to bring you down to their level and negate the positive tone you have set at the start of the day.

Maintaining a positive daily tone also calls for consideration of how you answer your telephone. Think of all the people you call who answer their phones the same way— either apprehensively or as if they're ill. You sometimes get the feeling that they're expecting every call to bear bad news. Contrast this to people who answer their phone in a bright, cheerful, and effervescent manner. Using this more positive approach pays dividends, both in the way you think and feel and the way your callers respond to you.

Zig Ziglar discusses this issue at length in his seminars and gives examples of unique, cheerful ways to answer the phone, such as, "Howdy, howdy. This is John Doe's happy wife! Who's this?" While such an unusual approach may not be suited for everyone, I'm sure you get the idea and can adapt an appropriately positive telephone greeting that fits your personality and style.

An added benefit of positive telephone greetings at home is that they are quickly picked up by the children. You'll soon see them thinking, acting, and feeling the same way. You may also discover that your creative uniqueness in this and other areas attracts more and more of the neighborhood children to your house. You won't have to wonder where your child is, because he or she will be at home.

Another benefit of daily positive thinking is the ability to avoid the use of victim language. See if you can go the whole day without making an "I can't...," "I have to...," "I wish...," or "I'll try..." statement. Instead, use positive phrases like "I have decided to...," "I want to...," "I can...," or "I will..." If you normally "doodle" while on the phone, in meetings, or waiting someplace, try writing "I can..." or "I will..." affirmations instead of your normal doodles. Make it a game for family members to monitor each other and catch any victim language usage. Have a reward for when a certain time limit is surpassed without the use of victim language. The more you practice not using victim language, the more you'll feel in control. And if you can maintain such thinking for the magical 21 to 28 day period, you'll find the new thought process is becoming permanently ingrained in your subconscious as well as your conscious mind.

Avoiding obvious victim language gradually results in feeling more responsible for all your thoughts and actions. You can then learn to spot and avoid less obvious, but nevertheless self-defeating, blameful statements, such as "I never learned to do that; my mother always did it for me" or "My supervisor insulted me, so I quit" or "I can't help it; that's the way my dad is" or a real favorite that we've all heard and said, "I just haven't had the time to do it yet" when what we really mean is "I haven't *taken* the time..."

As you move from negative, blaming statements to more positive, responsibility-oriented thinking, you also need to praise yourself, often and liberally. Focus on good qualities while downplaying undesirable attributes. It's just as important to recognize your own self-worth and good attributes as it is to praise others. Statements such as "I like that paint job on the house" or "I did a great job organizing the garage" or "I look good in this dress" or "I dealt with her so effectively, I'm proud of myself" can all be effective. This kind of legitimate self-praise needs to be done in the presence of your child whenever possible. This is the best and quickest way for him or her to learn the same behavior.

As self-praise develops into a normal trait, you will learn to accept the compliments of others simply and graciously. It's best to just say "Thank you!" Avoid the use of critical comments or qualifiers like "I could have done better if I'd had more time" or "I didn't have much to work with, so that's why it's a little rough."

Once you can fully accept yourself in this manner, you can find ways to improve your relationships and raise the self-esteem of others. When you do that, you simultaneously raise your own feeling of self-worth.

One of the simplest ways to show your acceptance of others is to smile at them. Another sure method is to praise them. But the praise should be specific—"You did a great job on the Jones' report!" rather than "You are a great report writer!" Praise should be given immediately after the act and not delayed. For best results, the praise should be intermittent and unpredictable; effectiveness is invariably lost when praise is given too liberally and regularly. By praising only that which you want in or from another person, you greatly enhance the likelihood that this will continue to be the output produced.

By focusing on things to praise in others, you can also avoid arguments. Arguments only say to the other person, "You are wrong!" This message lowers feelings of importance and self-worth.

A better approach, more consistent with a winning attitude, is to employ an imaginary or "straw" person in potentially argumentative situations. Try something like "What would you say if..." or "That's a strong reason, but (name) would counter it with..." This allows someone else to carry your torch for you, forcing your adversary to argue with someone who's not there. As a result, they are more apt to back down if they can be convinced.

> *If I have the belief that I can do it,*
> *I shall surely acquire the capacity*
> *to do it, even if I may not*
> *have it at the beginning.*

Another way to build other people up and make them feel more important is to listen attentively to them. Winners know that this entails such learned skills as (a) looking the other person squarely in the face, (b) pausing slightly before replying so as to show the other person you're carefully considering their viewpoint or message, (c) asking questions when necessary for clarification, and (d) feeding back your interpretations of their main points or issues to ensure that you've got them clear.

One more practice to generate positive thinking is to focus more on what you desire instead of what you fear. Fear triggers negative emotions. Desire is the real soul food;

it's the best long-term motivator because it presents little or no risk. Since you can only focus effectively on one main thought at a time, the more you focus on your desires, the more negative emotions are prevented from entering your day-to-day life.

Affirmations And Visualizations.
Highlights

- ✧ *All top performers use affirmations and visualizations to help reach their goals.*
- ✧ *Affirmations are simple positive statements like "I am a non-smoker" or "I eat only healthy foods."*
- ✧ *Visualizing involves forming a clear mental picture of what you want to do, have, be, or achieve.*
- ✧ *Autogenic conditioning techniques make visualization even more effective.*
- ✧ *Affirmations and visualizations should always follow the three Ps: personal, positive, and present.*
- ✧ *The first and last hours of each day are the most effective times for stating affirmations and practicing visualizations.*
- ✧ *You should use affirmations and visualizations often.*

To focus fully on what you desire and unleash the goal-seeking guidance of your subconscious mind, you must *internalize* the reasons and rewards behind the desire. This internalization is done through affirmations and visualizations.

Using affirmations to replace victim language, as discussed in the previous section, is an important aspect of generating positive thinking. But how do you build an effective affirmation? First, it should always adhere to the three Ps: **personal, positive, and present.**

Personal means it must be an "I" statement rather than a "you" statement. Remember, a goal or change must be your own. It won't work for you if it applies to someone else.

Positive means it doesn't involve any negative thoughts. Research has shown that we have much less success when we put negative thoughts or the reverse of an idea into our minds. Picture this illustration: We're in the final inning of the final game of the World Series. The score is tied when the final batter steps up to the plate; he's known to be a real slugger of high, outside fastballs. The manager walks briskly out to the mound and cautions the pitcher, "Don't give 'em a high, outside fastball."

Can you guess the outcome? Whack! The game's over— the *unwanted* pitch becomes the pitch delivered, which becomes a home run. Reverse motivation all too frequently works—in delivering just the opposite of what is desired. So keep your affirmations positive: "I throw him an inside curve ball." Similarly, "I am a non-smoker" is better than "I will not smoke again." "I only eat healthy foods" is much more effective than "I don't eat fats and sugars."

Present means that your affirmation is stated in the present, "now" tense. Start your affirmation with "I **do**...," "I **am**...," "I **have**...," "I **earn**...," and so forth.

Affirmations are a powerful tool and one of the real keys to success if properly stated and used. They can be used to propel us towards anything we want to obtain or to accomplish. But they need to be said with confidence, belief, and sincerity. Also, since they must be driven deep into our subconscious minds, our affirmations need to be repeated over and over, always adhering to the three Ps—personal, positive, and in the present tense.

Another key for putting our affirmations to work is to accompany them with visualizations. As we discussed in the chapter on goal-setting, top-performing men and women in all areas of life—from business to sports to the field of science—use visualizations. And as we learned in goal-setting, visualizations are most effective if we make them as detailed as possible and incorporate scenes which involve emotions.

Consider this true story about Liberace, the renowned pianist. His great dream had always been to play before a full house at the Hollywood Bowl. So he secretly rented the Bowl, had a piano delivered, and then, telling no one, sat and played to the imaginary crowd. He visualized the crowd's response in all its glory, clapping and cheering. A scant 3 years later, the real event occurred just as he had pictured it.

Top performers often rehearse their visualizations daily. The most effective times, in order of preference, are at night just before going to sleep, first thing in the morning, and any other time we have "down" time. Down time may happen on the way to work, during lunch, while waiting for an appointment, whenever we're not otherwise specifically occupied.

Examples of what people have achieved through their visualizations are impressive, if not downright astonishing. Most near-perfect and record-setting sports accomplishments began with the perfect visualization of that specific goal actually being accomplished.

When some of our Vietnam War prisoners returned home after long years of confinement, they could play professional-level golf, piano, or guitar, despite never having tried these endeavors before. How did they achieve such excellence? They simply *practiced* in their minds, using their visualizations.

I remember my own recent impressive example. Faced with having to give what I knew would be an unpopular speech to a large, mostly adversarial group (who were, incidentally, of higher rank and power than I), I found my stomach getting knotted and nervous. But for two evenings before the fateful day, I retreated to a quiet part of the house and went through the whole affair in my mind's eye. I saw myself calmly and professionally delivering my message with all of its detail and rationale. I also saw some of the adversarial heads around the table nodding in agreement, as if to compliment me on the *way* I delivered the message, if not the message itself. And, not wanting to leave myself open to the sharp questioning this deliverance was sure to bring, I anticipated beforehand all the hard questions, prepared answers to them, and then made sure I covered them in the speech. The actual outcome was just as I had pictured in the practice runs: a calm, polite, and respectful acceptance of my presentation—and not a single difficult question at the end.

A rational thinker can have a hard time accepting the mind's ability to control actions and events. But the mind-body connection has been demonstrated scientifically. For example, some years ago, several researchers studied what went on in the brain when it was having an "experience." The subjects were connected to EEGs (electroencephalographs), which measure brain waves. First, they were introduced to actual experiences, including a gunshot, a woman's scream, and a dog running across the room. Later, they were asked to visualize these same experiences. Surprisingly, the brain waves recorded from the two kinds of stimuli were identical, suggesting that our attitudes, habits, and responses to an imagined experience may be the same as for the real experience.

The value of imagery has been validated literally hundreds of times in research into the performance of motor skills. One recent example is a study conducted at the University of Chicago exploring the effects of visualization on basketball foul-shooting success. The subjects were divided into three groups: Group 1 actually practiced foul-shooting every day for an hour; Group 2 came to the gym, lay down on the floor, and "saw" themselves making successful foul shots for an hour; Group 3 did nothing and were actually told to "forget about basketball." At the end of 30 days on these regimes, everyone's starting foul-shooting proficiency was reexamined. The individuals who were told not to think about basketball either remained the same or dropped in performance. Those actually shooting every day showed an average success increase of 24 percent. What really surprised everyone was that those who simply *imagined* their shots for 1 hour daily had essentially the same success increase—23 percent!

The common denominator for all imagery, and a basic guideline for each of us, is to simply form a clear mental picture of the thing we want to *do, have, be,* or *achieve.* Whatever we can hold in our minds on a sustained basis becomes our self-propelling prophecy. But we must see ourselves as *already having* the attribute. We need to also use the same three Ps—personal, positive, and present—as discussed for affirmations. And finally, we need to include in the mental picture as much detail and emotion as we can.

One of the more advanced visualization approaches has been referred to as **autogenic conditioning**. It's widely used by former Eastern Bloc countries for programming for sports achievements. It's also what I used in the adversarial speech example I gave earlier. Although a more detailed discussion of this approach is given later on in the Stress Reduction chapter, here's basically how it works: First, find a quiet spot where you won't be disturbed; this means no children, phones, TV, barking dogs, roadway traffic noise, or whatever else might distract you. Next, lie down, close your eyes, and begin to relax deeply and completely. Slowly count down from 50 to 1, with each count on a full, deep breath. Now, go through your visualization(s) as described above. For best results, apply this routine either during the first or last hour of your day.

Writing down your goals and affirmations can also greatly facilitate visualization techniques. Just remember to write them clearly and specifically, with as much detail as possible. And again, always follow the three Ps, and do the writing either at the beginning or ending of your day, so your subconscious mind will drive your actions all day. Rewriting goals and affirmations regularly drives them deeper and deeper into your subconscious. This gets you to the place where you are as unstoppable as a cruise missile headed for the target.

Denying Negative Emotions.
Highlights

✦ *Negative emotions are like the branches of a large tree.*

✦ *To kill the tree and prevent negative emotions from taking over your life, attack the roots or trunk, not the individual branches.*

✦ *Eliminate destructive criticism from your language.*

✦ *Avoid blame by forgiving, especially your parents.*

✦ *Look for the good in any adverse situation.*

✦ *Treat problems as challenges that have logical, workable solutions.*

✦ *Analyze big challenges and worries on paper and then take appropriate action.*

✦ *When you kill the negative emotion tree, you can move unimpeded towards your goal.*

Invariably our most successful affirmations and visualizations are based on what we *desire* and not on what we *fear*. Our minds can only work on one dominant, major thought at a time, so the more we focus on our desires, which are the real soul food of our lives, the less chance we have of being burdened with negative emotions.

But even the highest achievers are sometimes troubled by this malady. An essential component of the winning attitude is understanding how to deal with negative emotions when they start raising their ugly heads.

Brian Tracy, a superb motivational speaker and psychologist, likes to view negative emotions as a large tree with branches (the 50 or more negative emotions), a trunk, and roots. If we want to kill the negative emotion tree, it's best to go after either the roots or the trunk.

The trunk can be viewed as blame. If we cut out blame, which is equivalent to girdling the trunk, we kill the tree. When faced with a situation that would otherwise elicit our negative emotions (for example, our anger or fear towards a tailgating driver), we can simply accept the responsibility for the volatile situation. The situation is immediately defused when we blame ourselves instead of someone else. We girdle the trunk of the negative emotion tree and kill it.

This approach is consistent with the **Law of Cause and Effects** mentioned earlier. It isn't easy the first time we do it, but it becomes easier with each repetition.

I also mentioned earlier that there's an important exception to this concept. The exception is this: Never blame yourself for the way your child has turned out. Accept the situation as reality, realize that you did the best you could at the time, and vow to move forward and improve upon past mistakes, using your newfound knowledge.

What about the other way to kill the negative emotion tree—eliminating the roots? Clearly, one of the primary roots is destructive criticism. Winners learn to eliminate it from their talk. They don't beat up on themselves, and they don't use destructive criticism on others. You won't catch them making these kinds of statements:

"Look at her! Did you ever see anybody so clumsy?" (I'm so clumsy.)

"Charlie sure has his brother's stubbornness; there's no use trying to reason with him!" (I've got my brother's stubbornness.)

"How come you're so dumb!" (I'm so dumb.)

"Can't you say anything that makes sense?" (I can't say anything that makes sense.)

"That's the way, keep eating. You already look like a blimp!"
(I really look like a blimp.)

Having a winning attitude means that you *know* this kind of talk, if used repeatedly on yourself or others, can reduce chances for success. Unfortunately, there are millions of examples throughout our society which prove it.

You have to wonder how many times a variation of this sad story has been played out: Jason is doing poorly in school. His teacher, with the best of intentions, advises him that he's "just not academically suited" and should quit and go to a trade school "where you'll be better off." So Jason quits and resigns himself to a life of mediocrity. Much later, however, through a series of fortunate events, Jason discovers that he really has an IQ of 162 and almost unlimited potential. His life turns around. How much better it would have been to avoid the early destructive criticism, focus on his positive points, and thereby provide the nurturing that would have helped Jason discover his true potential—15 years sooner.

Winners also know that it's best to avoid holding grudges and bitterness against others. Giving up and letting go of grudges and bitterness is another very effective way to kill the negative emotion tree—by going for its roots. It's an excellent sign of a healthy personality.

The first people we should totally forgive are our parents. Most of us have deep, unresolved anger or bitterness towards one or both of our parents. It may be something specific they did or didn't do, or their general failure to convey their love to us. Whatever the root or cause, it can be eliminated by simply forgiving them and accepting that they, too, did the best they could with what they had at the time.

Does it matter *how* we do this? Not really. We can discuss it with them in person. We can call or simply write a letter or note. For each of us, the effect is usually the same: a feeling—sometimes quite overwhelming—of relief and a greater ability to get on with reaching our full potential as human beings. Giving up the bitterness against our parents allows us to begin to see them as human beings and friends.

The same approach can be taken with all the others who have ever hurt us. Simply forgive and let the bitterness go. Wipe the slate clean. It doesn't mean we have to love them, like them, or even associate with them; it only means that we forgive and let it pass.

Having wiped the slate clean with our parents and all others, it's easier to do the same with ourselves. We need to accept that it's natural that we made mistakes in the past.

Another effective way to kill the negative emotion tree is to "look for the good." This means that, whatever the crisis, adversity, or problem that faces us, we analyze it and find the good. No matter what the adversity, there is always a good point, too. Start by asking yourself, "What has it *taught* me? What has it *made* me do? What other *actions* has it triggered?" The more you ask such questions and look for the good, the easier it becomes to find good in your adversities.

I have personally found the "looking for the good" method an extremely powerful tool, and I use it frequently. The depth or severity of the adversity doesn't matter. It can be something as trivial as having an argument or getting a traffic citation, or as burdensome as a death in the family or the loss of a relationship. Whatever the negative event, we can kill the negative emotion tree by focusing on the good that's created by it.

You can take a similar tack with problems, no matter how big or small. How you treat the problem determines whether the roots of the negative emotion tree are fertilized or killed. Winners learn that they can kill the roots with a three-pronged approach to problems. First, they never refer to anything as "a problem." They look at it as a "situation" or a "challenge." Right away, this approach hacks off a few of the roots of the negative emotion tree. Next, winners understand and accept that every situation or challenge has a logical, workable solution. This thought results in more roots being snipped away.

> ## *Problems are only opportunities in work clothes.*

And finally, winners know that if the situation or challenge is particularly big and troublesome, they need to sit down and *analyze* it on paper. They write down all the possible outcomes, including the *worst* one. This "zaps" a few more roots of the negative emotion tree, because invariably big challenges never seem as troublesome and fearful when they are reduced to a few written words on a page.

After writing down all the possible solutions to a challenge, you need to implement one. Taking action is one of the most effective ways of killing the remaining roots of the negative emotion tree.

Your friend, the subconscious mind, is there to help when you use this step-by-step approach to solving problems. When you can't decide on the particular course of action to take, or when the options themselves are not clear, sleep on it. At night, your subconscious mind will continue to work. Be ready with a pen and paper. Big thoughts, ideas, and solutions are likely to jump out and wake you up. When this happens, write them down quickly. You don't want to forget them, and acknowledging them helps you go back to sleep without worrying about remembering the thought.

Since I've brought up worry, let's talk about it for a moment. Worry is really a form of fear sustained by indecision. Basically, it amounts to negative goal-setting. It is also one of the most prevalent maladies in today's society and one of the biggest branches on the negative emotion tree.

To eliminate the basis for worry, deal with it just like a situation or challenge. Sit down with paper and pen, then write out exactly what you're worried about. Be specific and detailed. About half the time, that alone will do it! You'll gain relief by reducing the worry down to a few words on a page.

If you still have some worry feelings, take the second step: Write down in detail the worst-possible outcome. Resolve to *accept* this worst-possible scenario if it occurs. Lastly, write down and then take all the actions you can to prevent this worst-possible outcome from occurring.

Ninety percent of the time, as soon as you make decisions to *act* regarding your worries, the fear, tension, and stress begin to subside. This systematic written approach practically guarantees that the roots of worry are eliminated, or at least greatly reduced.

> *Confronting a problem doesn't always bring a solution, but until you confront the problem, there can be no solution.*

Overcoming Procrastination.
Highlights
✧ *Begin now, starting with the most important part.*
✧ *Action generates motivation.*

As we learn to control worry and other branches of the negative emotion tree and develop other aspects of a winning attitude, we also diminish the malady of procrastination. But based on my own life experiences, including the long time it took me to really begin this book, I'd say that we never totally free ourselves from the malady.

> ## *Procrastination is the thief of time.*

There are effective countermeasures, however, to the problem of procrastination. One simple trick is to start a task or project immediately. Another is to go after the most important first and do it with a sense of urgency. Admittedly, only about 2 percent of us can follow such advice. You can improve your odds, however, through affirmations like "I do it now!" Those who follow this mind-set are capable of outperforming smarter, better-educated people.

Just getting started can make a tremendous difference. In his book, *Feeling Good, The New Mood Therapy,* David D. Burns, M.D., explains that "motivation does not come first, *action* does! You have to prime the pump. If you wait until you're "in the mood," you may wait forever. When you don't feel like doing something, you tend to put it off, but getting involved in a task will often generate motivation to complete it.

> ## *Do it now!*
> ## *Today will be yesterday tomorrow.*

Job Ethics, Habits, And Appearance.
Highlights

    ✧ *Many people perform their jobs in mediocre fashion.*

    ✧ *Winners know that achieving job excellence results in*

job security.

✧ *Job excellence is facilitated by:*
  ✧ *a clean desk or work area;*
  ✧ *daily goals lists for high productivity;*
  ✧ *a good appearance, along with a straight walk and clear talk.*

✧ *Winners are willing to pay the price to get the job they want.*

A majority of our population goes through their entire lives doing their jobs in just an average, mediocre fashion. This is especially true of those with low self-esteem and self-image. They never seem to learn how important it is to attain excellence at what they do for a living.

Winners know it though! Part of the winning attitude is to remember that *we* applied for the job; our employers didn't come seeking us out, unless we have already achieved excellence in our field.

> *One employer was asked: "How many people do you have working for you?" The reply was, "Oh, about half of them."*

The winning attitude also means that we don't steal from or cheat our employers "to make up for the lousy pay" or "to get even for the poor working conditions" or simply because "they *owe* me." And it means that if we have a problem with the job, we leave and move on to a better job.

With a winning attitude, we regularly analyze our job situation to determine "what more I can *give* to *get* what I want."

Having a winning attitude about our job and achieving the maximum level of job excellence we are capable of attaining ensure job security. The economic climate or job conditions in our chosen field don't matter. It has been shown again and again that the top one-third of workers in any particular classification, in any given field, are *always* assured of jobs, regardless of trends in that field.

> ## *Your rewards in life will always match your service.*

You can spot the winners who are always assured of jobs not only by their attitudes but by their *appearance* and the appearance of their work spaces. A disorganized, messy desk or work space typifies a person whose energies are being dissipated; it reveals one who flits from task to task, never focusing in depth or completing to perfection any one item. A clean desk or work area signifies that the person focuses, works faster, and works more efficiently.

Here's a good rule to follow that is practiced by most top business executives: Look at each piece of paper that comes before you and make a decision about it, right then and there. Delegate it for further action, file it, or discard it. But never look at that same piece of paper twice. Your fidelity to such a simple rule will always keep your desk clear.

Here's another simple rule that can be adapted to an even wider range of job situations. When you arrive at your desk or work space each morning, write down from one to six of the most important things you must do. Then vow to do the items, in that order, without letting anyone or anything distract you until they are accomplished. This type of daily goal-setting generates a tremendous increase in productivity and accomplishments.

And now to the issue of personal *appearance* on the job. It's an enigma that so many people believe they do no damage or harm when they dress or appear abnormal compared to the norm for their jobs. But abnormal appearance often shows that the person is responding to some outside peer group; this tends to signify lack of control over one's life. Winners know not to put the wrong message into their subconscious minds. You become what you think about. If you come to work looking weird or abnormal, you're inclined to think and act that way. If you're serious about climbing the ladder of success, avoid looking abnormal.

The same goes for other aspects of your demeanor at work. For example, how you walk and talk can often be just as important as your dress. Losers often amble, shuffle, or use a peculiar gait. They may carry themselves with stooped shoulders or exhibit some other mark of a particular group or culture. Their talk may epitomize street savvy. In contrast, winners walk and talk straight and clear, using the best of posture and English; they give the impression that they *know* exactly where they're going.

And when winners want a particular job, they're ready and willing to pay the price to get it. If it means starting at the bottom and working up, they do it. If it means volunteering and working for free to create the initial demand for themselves, they do it.

A shining example of the employment persistence ethic is the former disc jockey, community activist, Ohio legislator, motivational speaker, author, and now TV talk-show host Les Brown. Brown hasn't let anyone or anything turn him away from the jobs he wanted. Abandoned at 6 weeks of age and mislabeled as "educably mentally retarded" in the fourth grade, this 48-year-old man has made it to the top of several professions.

Though lacking in formal training, Brown initially attacked a very difficult goal: to get a job in radio "so I could buy my mamma a house." He pestered a local radio station owner for a job daily until he was hired as a "gofer." Between fetching coffee and chauffeuring celebrities, he watched, learned, and practiced his yet-to-be-unleashed on-air rap and personality. Then one day the right moment came. A disc jockey was too drunk to continue on the air, and Brown was asked to keep the records flowing until a replacement was found. He hit the airwaves with a vengeance and literally woke up the city.

An on-air controversy later got him fired, and the incident prevented him from getting another radio job. So he began listening to motivational speakers, learning their techniques and income possibilities. Through these observations and vigorous self-study (reading up to four books a week), this "educably retarded" man literally talked himself to the top of what was then a new field. Before his recent move to TV, he was commanding $10,000 and more a piece for up to 200 90-minute training and motivational seminars a year for executives of Xerox, IBM, General Electric, AT&T, and other Fortune 500 companies.

Planning And Time Management.
Highlights

- ✧ *You need to make specific plans to achieve your goals.*
- ✧ *Unbudgeted time, like unbudgeted money, slips away with little memory for where it went.*
- ✧ *Make daily activity lists, prioritize them, and focus on one item at a time to achieve your goal.*

Good planning and good time management always go hand in hand with a winning attitude. As we learned earlier in the goal-setting section, winners develop a plan and stick to it. They know they can achieve or obtain anything they want in life by using a systematic, step-by-step planning approach. They know that, without a plan, they are like a ship without a rudder or a car without a steering wheel—hopelessly adrift and at the mercy of the terrain. Planning is an essential step in programming our goals for success. (Note: If you're rereading this section, it's a good idea to also review either the nine-step process for goal programming beginning on page 99 or the highlights of that section on page 98.)

Winners learn, however, that careful planning alone doesn't guarantee reaching the goal. Another essential ingredient is time management; we must manage our time efficiently and effectively. Unbudgeted time is like unbudgeted money; it tends to slip away, and we wonder where it went. Time spent on keeping track of how we spend our time is well spent. This is true for both the goals we are pursuing and in our jobs.

There are numerous courses and books on time management available, but the gist of their message focuses on four key elements:

1. Have goals and a plan for achieving them. This is the overall guide that tells you where you're going and how you're going to get there.

2. Use daily activities lists. These provide guidance for each day. Make a list each evening for the next day. This will "sweep your mind clean" and allow you a good night's sleep. The next morning, refuse to do anything that's not on your list. If a new obligation arises, put it on the list (this immediately lessens its significance) but delay it if possible. At the end of each day, make the next day's list, transferring any incomplete or unaddressed items to the new list.

Using daily lists gives you a feeling of accomplishment and being in control. Without such lists, you're more likely to respond and invest your time on the urgent rather than the truly important.

3. Set priorities on these lists. Experience shows that 75 to 90 percent of the total value on these lists is contained in 10 to 20 percent of the items. It's important to set priorities. If you can't complete the entire list, the least valuable items are dropped. An easy way to set priorities is to ask yourself, "If I could only do *one* thing tomorrow, what would it be?" If the list has multiple items, keep doing this (i.e., "... one more thing") until you have established a priority sequence.

4. Stick with each item on the list until it's done. Focus single-mindedly on one thing at a time, ensuring it is completely done. Then, and only then, should you move on to the next item on the list.

CHAPTER 13

Nurturing Self-Esteem and Self-Image

Highlights

✧ *Feeling capable and loved builds self-esteem.*

✧ *Work to instill these feelings in your children.*

Here's an important formula worth remembering: Self-esteem = Feelings of Capability + Feelings of Lovability. It would be difficult to overstate the importance of this relationship.

Authorities have estimated that up to half of the people entering doctors' offices for care of a physical disorder or disease—even for surgery—have more of a psychological problem than a physical ailment. Many of these people are suffering from the effects of low self-esteem and its attendant maladies.

One of the most powerful determinants of any given child's self-esteem and self-image is the degree that these attributes are developed in the primary adult caregiver. This should be of little surprise. We can't expect to give something to our children that we ourselves do not possess. That's why much of this book deals directly or indirectly with developing healthy self-esteem in the adolescent or adult.

But to make the discussion complete, we need to now focus specifically on the child. We need to learn about the specific, positive things that parents can and should do to ensure that their child develops a healthy self-esteem and self-image. Much of this discussion will be centered around two four-letter words: L-O-V-E and T-I-M-E.

Love.
Highlights

- ✧ *Tell your child often that you love him or her.*
- ✧ *Provide hugging and other nurturing physical contact daily.*
- ✧ *Give your child frequent direct and loving eye contact.*
- ✧ *Don't offer your child conditional love.*
- ✧ *As parents, show a model of love and affection, not physical or verbal abuse.*

Nothing is more important to a child's feelings of self-worth than the knowledge that he or she is loved unequivocally by *both* parents. Many of the other mistakes parents make with their child can be overcome if this one condition is met. Love is as essential to the child as sunshine to plants, flowers to bees, and raindrops to the rivers.

Too many uninformed parents mistakenly *assume* that their acts of kindness, support, feeding, and otherwise dutiful caring for their child demonstrate their love for that child. But this is far from true. Picture Golde in *Fiddler on the Roof.* She's asked by her husband, "Do you love me?" Her reply: "What a foolish question! I've washed your clothes, cooked your food, and borne your children for 25 years!"

Her husband persists: "But I just want to know if you *love* me?" After a few more tries, he finally elicits from her a qualified "I suppose I do."

Children must never be subjected to such doubts or examples of qualified love. They must hear us say that we love them, and hear it often!

If parents haven't made a practice of saying "I love you" to their children, starting to do it may confuse them— especially teenagers. They may perceive the words as sarcastic or an attempt at manipulation. However, if you persist, they will see that you are sincere. You may be surprised at the improved attitudes of other family members from this one self-esteem-boosting measure.

We need to show as well as tell our children we love them. For example, if a child—especially an adolescent—isn't getting at least six to ten hugs a day, he or she is probably "undernourished." Some experts believe that the minimum threshold for basic survival is four daily hugs.

Eye contact with a child is equally important. It's a tragedy that so many parents fail to do this. Too often, the most prevalent eye-to-eye contact is when we scold or reprimand. What is needed is direct, loving eye contact for as prolonged periods as possible. Infants respond to such nurturing starting at 6 weeks of age. Few other actions so miraculously recharge the drained emotional tanks of a child as direct, loving eye contact from a parent.

Babies can see clearly and with discrimination from the moment of birth. But their visual range is limited because they are extremely nearsighted. A baby's fixed focal distance does not seem to be a random matter. It is the exact distance between the baby's face and that of the parent who is holding, talking to, or nursing him or her. Just as talk and touch are critical needs, so too is the parent's face, accompanied by direct eye contact.

As explained in a chapter in The Maladies That Limit Us, another component of the love formula is to avoid the use of conditional love. Far too many parents mistakenly employ this very effective way to control their child's behavior. Although behavior may be temporarily steered in a desired direction, the toll on the child's feelings of confidence, lovability, and self-esteem is tremendous. Children need to know that their parents love them whether their behavior is acceptable or not. Parents must separate children from their actions and let them know that, while their actions are disliked, they are still loved. In line with this, it's not a bad idea to tell your child he or she is loved immediately after a spanking or other form of punishment or discipline. Make sure your child gets the correct message: "Mommy loves you, but that was wrong."

> ## *One father is worth a thousand school masters.*

Another vital component of the love formula is for a child to see love and affection being displayed between the parents. It has been said that the greatest gift a man can give to his children is the knowledge that he loves their mother; it is undoubtedly just as important for them to know that their mother loves their father. The child needs to see the parents holding hands, kissing, and otherwise displaying their affection. This provides security and a feeling of being loved, too. It also provides a model for the child to follow later. All children need to learn to display feelings of love and affection.

No child should see parents physically or verbally abusing each other. This lowers the child's self-esteem and lays the groundwork for similar treatment of his or her own mate in adulthood. In a good marriage, each partner outwardly loves and supports the other, speaks well of the mate, and each defends the other against the outside world. These are the ideal messages of love that the developing child so vitally needs.

> ### *Marriage is not looking at each other but looking in the same direction together.*

Time.
Highlights

✧ *Spend one-on-one time with your child daily.*

✧ *You can do this by involving your child in more things you have to do.*

✧ *Any mutual activities must be enjoyable to both you and your child.*

✧ *Use family meals for relaxed communication and inter-action.*

✧ *The other best times to spend with your child are first thing in the morning and at bedtime.*

✧ *Be sure to accommodate a toddler's need for more attention when a new baby joins your household.*

T-I-M-E is closely intertwined with L-O-V-E in the self-esteem equation. Many parents know that they must spend "quality" time every day with their children. But how many parents really *understand* the concept of quality time? And how many know what's acceptable and what isn't?

An occasional 10-minute "enrichment period" with the parent will rarely fulfill a child's basic needs. And the mere presence of adults and older children in the home doesn't guarantee that significant child/adult interactions are occurring. A parent engrossed in a newspaper or cooking dinner can be just as inaccessible to the child as if he or she is out of town.

Especially in today's two-wage-earner homes, one or both parents may be inclined to think, "I realize I'm not spending enough time with Jody and Mark, but it's all I can do to meet all my other obligations. Where am I going to find the time?" Statistics show that this dilemma is widespread. The average U.S. father spends only 2 quality minutes a week with each of his prepubescent children and 7 quality minutes a week with each teenage child.

One solution is to find more things to involve your children in that you would be doing anyway. For example, young children may love to go to the store, the bank, the post office, or to mommy's work place if you have errands to conduct there. Taking them along can lessen the dilemma of limited time.

As a child gets older, going to the store with mommy or daddy loses its appeal. But it's still critically important for the older child to spend time with parents. Develop other mutual interests with your child at this point. Movies, trips to amusement parks, shopping trips, various crafts or hobbies, or any number of sports activities, such as fishing, hunting, and ball games, are all potential outlets.

Make sure that the time you spend together is mutually enjoyable. It you're constantly looking at your watch and thinking of other things on your list, your child will sense it. You won't stimulate growth of self-esteem if he or she knows you're there out of a sense of duty.

The best way to ensure the child knows you *want* to be with him or her is to communicate whenever you're together. And the first principle of such communication is to *listen* with undivided attention to the child. Parents too often listen with only one ear, while the other ear is tuned to the TV, telephone, or some other conversation. We are often so concerned about injecting our "2 cents worth" into a conversation or deciding how to frame our thoughts into words that we fail to listen closely to our children as well as others.

The vast majority of parents can benefit from remaining silent and listening more to their children. This allows us to learn how our children think, reason, and view the world. And when we listen, our children feel more accepted, understood, and worthwhile.

In listening to and communicating with our children, we may need to exercise caution that we don't become their servants, however. Consider this situation with Mr. Hill: He's talking with a neighbor or friend, and one of his children interrupts the conversation. He stops in the middle of a sentence and turns all his attention to the child. This is taking things too far. The child deserves the same privileges as all other people, including adults, but not more. Obviously, the better approach is to teach the child how to trigger being brought into adult conversations in a controlled manner.

While time spent communicating one-on-one with your child is important, so is time spent communicating together as a family unit. Family events may include outings to movies, sporting events, amusement parks, or any place that commonality exists. The daily family meals are especially important. This can be a time for relaxed interactions and discussions among family members, and it provides a form of order that is vitally important to the developing child's self-esteem.

But what can a parent do if work schedules prevent regular interactions at family meals? The parent should then focus on the two other most important times of the day: when the child first arises and at bedtime.

Psychologists have found that the first input that the child receives each day is usually more important than the next five encounters. That's why it's best to be present when your child arises, so you can provide a loving, nurturing, affection-filled encounter. Plan enough time to avoid rushing to school or the daycare provider, even if it requires adjusting your schedule and getting up earlier each morning. The benefits are well worth the effort.

Bedtime is equally important. Bedtime should be a quiet, peaceful time for both of you to "wind down" from the day's bustle of activities. Reading to or listening to the child read, playing quiet games, singing songs, or talking about some event of the day can all be effective self-esteem builders. Such activities also facilitate a sound, restful night's sleep for the child.

Admittedly, most children will at times balk at the thought of going to bed. It may seem unfair that older siblings can stay up or that a particularly enjoyable activity can't be continued. Or the bedroom may trigger certain fears. For all of these reasons—as well as for building self-esteem—close parental contact at bedtime is essential. If there's more than one child, parents can stagger their bedtime duties with each nurturing a different child every night, or alternating the bedtime ritual with household duties.

One particular aspect of T-I-M-E management which deserves particular attention is the advent of a new baby into the family. Toddlers and young children require *more*, not less, attention at times like this. The distraught mother may be tempted to ask, "How can I give Erik *more* attention when the new baby takes almost *all* of my time?" This is when the father must get more involved by either spending more time with the toddler(s) while mom cares for the baby or caring for the baby so mom *does* have some time for the toddler(s).

There's another time where special caution is required. How often have you witnessed adults standing around a baby's crib oohing and ahing while the family's toddler(s) stood quietly in the background? If you're ever a visitor in such a household, don't forget to give some attention to the toddler(s) as well as the new baby. You might even want to bring the toddler(s) some small, inexpensive gifts.

The new mother can also help ease the situation by asking the toddler(s)—assuming they're old enough—to help in caring for the new baby.

Risk-Taking.
Highlights

✧ *The kind of risk-taking that develops high self-esteem is simply gathering experiences, not taking dangerous risks with your body or health.*

✧ *Use your surroundings, both inside and outside the house, as learning experiences for your child.*

✧ *Provide your child's surroundings with as few limits as possible.*

✧ *Minimize the use of negatives around your child.*

✧ *Focus on praising your child's accomplishments and avoid destructive criticism.*

✧ *Resist the urge to take over and do things for your child because you can do them quicker or better.*

In Chapter 10 I spoke about risk-taking and acceptance of failures. That was a generalized discussion to apply to everyone from toddlers to the elderly. Now, I want to focus on risk-taking as it applies to the young child. You may want to go back and reread the earlier chapter—or its summary—before reading this section.

Child development specialists have identified distinct periods when developmental readiness is highest. In particular, the peak period for motor development is ages 1 to 4. The peak period for intellectual development is from birth to age 3. And the peak period for rapid growth of self-esteem is from 6 to 18 months, although the building process continues much longer.

Throughout the peak period for building self-esteem, parents need to know the value of controlled risk-taking and let the child practice it as much as possible. (Remember, I'm not using risk-taking here or elsewhere to mean taking dangerous risks with your body or health.) The *kinds* of risk-taking allowed and encouraged vary with the child's readiness. Readiness progresses in sequences with individual variations. For example, most children learn to crawl before they walk; they learn words before phrases; they can take off their shoes and socks before they can put them on. We can pretty well *predict* the tasks our children are ready for by what they've already learned.

As any parent knows, we really don't need to *stimulate* risk-taking in a young child. They are going to be into everything—it's human nature!

Young children have so much to learn. What's amazing is how fast they do it. Be happy when children are inquisitive. Curiosity makes them better learners and more interesting people. But you may often get annoyed by the trouble and inconvenience that your child's natural curiosity brings.

The mother or father who thinks that the most important thing in the world is a clean, orderly house is usually in for trouble. The young child's natural tendency toward risk-taking negates cleanliness and order. What parents see as a child's attempt to "mess up the house" is only his or her exploration of how things work.

One good approach for the parent who can't stand the inevitable disorder is to maintain a particular room in the home where the child can play without limits. The other rooms can then be "child-proofed" by putting expensive, breakable, irreplaceable, and dangerous items out of the child's reach and sight.

Above all, parents need to minimize their use of the words "no," "don't," and other negatives. Saying "no" often to a child has one of two effects: It either instills fear of trying or it has the opposite result, stimulating rebellious-ness. Here's a good rule to follow: Before you say no, ask yourself, "What difference does it *really* make?" Many times, there's not a good justification for denying the activity in question.

What I've just said applies to the young and very young child; these children are like Kamikaze pilots flying their aircraft off into the wild blue yonder. They don't need much encouragement to take risks. As children get older, the situa-tion changes and parents need to become more active in nurturing their children's inquisitiveness, boldness, and risk-taking.

When we teach our children to be bold, we don't need to encourage them to be reckless and foolhardy. We can simply encourage them to make deliberate decisions to try things they're not sure they can do—in other words, to risk failure. Is it better that we teach our children to aim high and occasionally fail than to shrink away from trying? Yes, an overwhelming body of research has shown this to be true! As children learn to confront things that pose risks, their experiences are broadened, their successes mount, and their self-esteem blossoms and grows.

> *Experience is not only the best teacher;*
> *it is often the only teacher.*

Children are going to be timid and anxious sometimes. Another important thing parents can teach them is that they never eliminate anxiety by avoiding the things that cause it. New and different things are by definition scary, but children can be taught, and come to believe, that they can't learn if they don't try. They also need to be taught that, as they persist at more and more scary things, fear subsides or may be eliminated altogether.

So what can you do within your home to foster boldness and learning in your child? For one thing, you can simply turn off the TV and talk to your child. You can look around your house and say, "See these pipes. This is where the water comes in. This is where the water goes out." You can go to the kitchen and cook a simple recipe for the child, step-by-step. You can look at family photo albums with him or her and talk about memories. You can weigh each other. You can go to the closet and sort out the used shoes and clothes you want to donate to charity. The opportunities are limitless. In short, you can help your child get excited about all the things in the house to learn about.

The same mind-set works when you take your child outside. For example, go for a walk and let your child take the lead. Allow plenty of time and remember that the more sensory stimulation he or she gets, the better. *Expect* the child to get dirty and possibly need a change of clothing when you get home. Children don't learn in a vacuum, and the more "hands-on" experience they get, the quicker they learn about the world and how to control it. With such learning, self-reliance and self-esteem flourish.

Nurturing boldness also necessitates avoiding destructive criticism. Focus instead on praising accomplishments.

Let's suppose that you come home from the grocery store and find that your beaming 6-year-old daughter has set the table for dinner. But the glasses are not matched and the silverware is out of order. Do you focus on these mistakes and tell the child why she *shouldn't* have *tried*? ("You're a little too young, sweetheart" or "It makes more work for mommy" or "You could have broken something!") Focusing on deficiencies serves only to deflate your child's ego and throw cold water on the thrill of her surprise for you.

Choose some other time to explain that it really looks nice when all the glasses are the same size, the forks are all on the left side, and so on. To nurture her boldness and risk-taking, thank her, say nothing about the errors, and focus on praising what was *good* about the effort.

Any time a child completes a job, the first natural adult tendency is to want to point out the weak areas, so the effort will be improved next time. But this is always more likely to discourage the effort than to make it better. If we focus on the parts well done, we preserve the child's delicate feelings of importance. If we always point out what's wrong, we gradually make the child believe he or she can't do *anything* right.

> ## *We don't even know that we've been imprisoned until we've broken out.*

Parents need to keep reminding themselves that their children cannot always perform at adult levels. When they've done their best, we need to praise the good wholeheartedly and avoid the temptation to show them how much better *we* could have done it.

While always looking for the good to praise, we need to also remember to restrain ourselves from taking over and doing things for our children just because we can do them better and faster. A mother's normal instinct might be to say to her 3-year-old child, "Let me pour the milk for you, honey! It's heavy and you might spill it." In reality, the risk posed, even if the milk is spilled, is small. And when the inevitable spill does occur, the wise parent can simply use the accident to provide another teaching opportunity as the child learns to clean it up.

Perhaps even worse than taking over and doing things children should be *trying* is discouraging children from even making the initial attempt. Consider the father who persuades his daughter not to try out for cheerleader because she has "no chance against all the prettier and more talented girls." Pity the young woman in college who refuses to wear shorts because she has "the world's ugliest legs." She's quite certain of this because when she was a child, her mother repeatedly told her so. These are the kinds of missiles of discouragement that unknowing parents can direct towards their children. Knowledgeable parents avoid them at all costs.

Knowledgeable parents are also careful not to compliment the physical attractiveness of *other* children in the presence of *their* children. Such an indirect message is often just as bad as a direct message of discouragement. Children soon believe that their parents place physical attractiveness above all else. They begin to feel inadequate. It's best to compliment other children in ways that don't focus on physical attractiveness: "Isn't she *well-behaved*?" or "Isn't he a *considerate* boy?"

So encouragement nurtures healthy self-esteem, but there still are potential dangers in teaching our children to be adventuresome and willing to take risks. For example, with this mind-set, they may experiment with drugs, alcohol, or antisocial dress and behaviors. But if they've developed high self-esteem, it's less likely that they will be sidetracked in these ways. And if they are, the excursions are more likely to be temporary and over quickly.

One of our goals in nurturing boldness and risk-taking in our children should be to make them feel confident and important. Dale Carnegie once suggested that we should visualize every person we encounter as having a large sign across their chest saying **"I want to feel important!"** To the extent we assist our children in meeting this basic need, we clearly enhance the development and growth of healthy self-esteem.

Decision-Making.
Highlights
❖ *Encourage your child to make as many decisions as possible.*

✧ *Allow your child to participate in family decision-making.*
✧ *These activities elevate the child's feelings of importance, intelligence, and responsibility, allowing self-esteem to blossom.*
✧ *To decide whether to let your child make a particular decision, simply ask yourself, "Can I live with the consequences no matter what the decision?"*

Just as we must refrain from taking over and doing physical things for our children, we must also avoid making too many decisions for them. Most parents make far more decisions than they should for their children. To do so gets them past immediate situations much quicker; but when you teach your children to make their own decisions, you foster higher self-esteem.

One key to developing good decision-making skills in your child is to set the example. Parents need to be seen as decisive. If you vacillate or become fretful over each decision, your child learns to act the same way.

> ### *What you do speaks so loudly, I cannot hear a word you say.*

For children, the transition from having parents make all of their decisions to making their own must be gradual. Children need to be allowed only the choices that are appropriate for their age. Infants have no capability to make decisions; everything must be decided for them. Toddlers gradually gain the ability for more and more simple decisions. And by late adolescence or early adulthood, children should be almost totally in charge of their own decisions and behaviors.

How do parents know which decisions can be delegated to children at any given age? One simple guideline is to not let them make decisions where an irresponsible choice could have dangerous consequences to them or others. Obviously, a 4-year-old child would not be allowed to choose to play in the street. Nor would a young child be allowed to choose to play outside during severely inclement weather.

> *He who is convinced against his will remains of the same opinion still.*

A second guideline is to ask yourself, "Am I prepared to accept and support the decision, regardless of what my child decides?" If your answer is yes, the decision can easily be delegated to the child.

Parents often violate this guideline, however. For example, they may say to a toddler "Should we go to bed now?" or "Do you want to come and eat now?" The typical child's answer is a resounding "No!" Since "No" is a decision the parent is not prepared to accept, it's better to say "It's bedtime" or "It's time for dinner" and then lead the toddler off to that activity.

In contrast, consider examples where the child's decision makes little or no difference to you: "Do you want to play inside or outside this afternoon?" (assuming that weather is not a factor) or "Do you want to wear your colored or plain pajamas to bed?" or "Should I read to you, or do you want to tell me a story?" or "Do you want to eat out of your plain bowl or your dinosaur bowl?"

As children advance in age, they can also be brought into family decision-making. You may choose to hold regular family meetings. This is a good way to share ideas, bring out problems for resolution, and discuss issues that affect all family members. Involving children in this process is an excellent means of fostering their feelings of importance. You don't have to give your children the ability to overrule or outvote you on issues. But they can have their views seriously and fully considered, especially on matters that may not make any significant difference to you (e.g., "Should we go to Disneyland or Yellowstone for vacation?" or "Which wallpaper should we put in the girls' room?")

The more you teach your children to make their own decisions and allow them a part in family decision-making, the more their feelings of importance, intelligence, and responsibility are elevated. As these rise, so do their feelings of self-esteem and good self-image.

Other Related Guidelines.
Highlights

✧ *Assertiveness, which is closely tied to risk-taking, means behaving boldy and confidently but in a calm, positive, and polite manner.*

✧ *Comparing one child to another isn't fair and can do a lot of damage to developing self-esteem.*

✧ *Recognize destructive criticism you have used in the past and apologize for it. Have the family monitor each other for such behavior.*

✧ *Give yourself a handicap in games or play games of chance so your child can experience winning.*

✧ *Boost your child's feeling of importance and self-esteem by attending his or her events.*

✧ *Teach your child appropriate dress, body language and posture to build confidence, self-worth, and performance.*

Let's quickly examine a few more things to remember about building healthy self-esteem in children:

1. Teach your child to be assertive. Assertiveness is closely related to risk-taking. But it's important to distinguish between assertiveness and aggressiveness. Assertiveness is behaving boldly and confidently but in a calm, positive, and polite manner. Aggressiveness entails the use of force, compulsion, and bad manners. Assertive people don't allow others to take unfair advantage, but neither do they exercise compulsion over others.

A very important area in which to build children's assertiveness is with respect to their bodies. They should always be taught that they have the right to resist requests or actions that they do not enjoy and which violate their values and rights. For example, they should be taught that no one, not even a parent, should touch them in personal places (these can be described as the parts covered by their underwear or swimming suit). They need to also be taught to be assertive in ensuring that no one displays these parts to them.

Your child's level of assertiveness can be enhanced just by displaying you own good assertiveness and decision-making abilities. It won't do for father to say, "Your *mother* doesn't want you to wear that dress," or mother to say, "You can go to the dance if your *father* says it's okay." Messages should always be directly from the speaking parent: *"I want you to..."* If you need to consult or collaborate with your spouse on a decision, do it out of the presence of your child.

2. Avoid comparing your child to a sibling or another child. I mentioned this earlier, but it's a key point that needs reemphasis. Always avoid these kinds of open and direct comparisons: "You'd be prettier if you did your hair like Polly" or "Why can't you behave like your brother?" or "If you practice every day, you may learn to play the piano as well as Cindy" or "Why can't you get straight As like your brother?"

It's never fair to expect a child to perform exactly like a sibling, especially an older one. Each child has his or her own unique set of talents and areas of excellence that should be developed and nurtured. The only thing that continued comparison brings about is the all-too-clear message: "I am not as capable, important, or lovable as my brother or sister." Over the long term, such messages do severe damage to a child's self-esteem, and the resulting problems may last a lifetime.

3. Make amends to your child for any past use of destructive criticism. Assuming that I've done my job well in this book, at this point you should be able to identify instances where *you've* employed destructive criticism against your child in the past. To heal the destructiveness, sit your child down, explain to him or her the instances, and admit that your behavior was wrong. Say you're sorry because destructive criticism lowers people's good feelings about themselves and their effectiveness. Give him or her permission to monitor you from now on. Point out that you should be told immediately if you ever use destructive criticism again. You could develop this idea into a game in which the whole family participates by monitoring each other. The desired outcome is to shift feelings of guilt related to the earlier criticisms from the child back to the parent. This will strengthen your child's character and build self-esteem.

4. Let the child win at games. Ever wonder if you should deliberately lose at games so your child feels the joy of winning with its attendant feelings of success? It's a good idea to control part of the outcomes so your child can win games or contests. Winning provides a big boost to feelings of importance.

One approach can be to give yourself a handicap—less money at the start of monopoly, left-handed catching or batting, less time on a video game. The need for such a handicap is usually short-lived—just long enough for your child's skills to develop. Soon enough, you may need to really go all out to win.

Another idea is to turn to games of chance, where skill and experience have no bearing on who wins or loses. That way, both of you automatically win some and lose some.

It's fun to win, but your child needs to learn that no one wins all the time. Everyone needs to learn to lose and to do so gracefully. It's also important for your child to see you win at times. If not, you could be viewed as inept, and that is not an image conducive to building your child's healthy self-esteem.

5. Attend your child's activities. Consider two typical adolescent girls—Ina and Karen. They are neighbors and close friends who attend the same school and participate in a wide range of activities. Whenever Ina is involved in some significant event, one or both of her parents are present to cheer her on. Karen's parents, on the other hand, don't feel that their presence at her events is all that vital; they're often "just too busy to attend." Through their failure to provide support, Karen's parents are missing easy ways to boost her feelings of importance and self-esteem.

Whenever your child is involved in any activity to which parents are invited, make a special effort to be there. Whether your son is on the second string or varsity team, whether your daughter is a soloist or just a member of the choir, show him or her that you consider the activities important. It's a given that such interest will inevitably boost your child's self-esteem.

6. Help your child to dress and act the part. How they dress, act, and present themselves is just as important for children as for adults. Children who are appropriately dressed perform better. It's a proven fact—dress the same child two different ways, and you'll get a significantly better performance associated with the better dress.

Also, teach your child the posture and body language

that bring respect from others. Much of our communication takes place without words. A child who slouches, scuffles or looks at the ground when walking, or avoids direct eye contact with others, sends out the wrong messages. As children learn to utilize appropriate posture and body language, their feelings of confidence and self-worth are enhanced, and their performance levels are invariably raised. One of the favorite bits of advice from the noted psychologist George Crane is, "Go through the proper *motions* and soon enough you'll begin to feel the corresponding *emotions*."

CHAPTER 14

Enhancing Creativity

Highlights
✧ *Creativity is often stifled in our children's lives by teachers and other significant people.*
✧ *Fortunately, creativity can always be reawakened at any age.*

Creativity is vital to high self-esteem and vice versa. Creativity is also closely tied to risk-taking; the more you have of one, the more you have of the other. Thus, the more you have done, seen, and tried, the more creative, effective, and happy you are likely to be.

Creativity involves originality of thought, the ability to break away from the norm and examine things in new, fresh ways. Opportunities to unleash creativity are everywhere; they can involve music, art, literature, science, our jobs, our everyday problem-solving—virtually anything that requires thought and concentration.

Creativeness cannot emanate from rigid, inflexible people. Unfortunately, most of us go through life being trained to be just that! Studies show that the greatest creativity in our children (in terms of abstract reasoning and creative imagery) occurs when they are between 2 and

4. By age 7, only about 4 percent of the original highly creative kids remain that way.

The problem is usually twofold: 1) children are too often "beaten back" by unknowledgeable parents who don't know and understand key principles for achieving success, and 2) our schools often stifle children's creativity. The problem with schools is that they concentrate on *convergent* thinking, where teachers pass on the accumulated wisdom of the past. They often fail to teach, or even allow, *divergent* thinking, where a child can go off on a tangent and think about things in new ways. Without divergent thinking, no new inventions or artistic achievements can occur.

Luckily, divergent thinking and creativity are never truly lost. They only become dormant from lack of use. There is much we can do to permanently instill creativity in the young child and to reawaken it in the older child or adult.

> *Be bold and mighty forces will come to your aid.*

The Young Child.
Highlights
- *Creative thinking and expression are as important as the three Rs.*
- *Creative success is more likely for children who develop interests of their own rather than being pushed into things.*
- *Enhance your child's opportunities for sparking creativity by:*
  - *keeping creative materials around the house;*
  - *finding something to praise in each creative effort;*

> ✧ *encouraging him or her to describe and engage in story-telling about creative efforts;*
> ✧ *learning with your child instead of always being the teacher.*

Most research gravitates towards one common conclusion: Creative success—regardless of the field—is more likely for children who develop *their own* interests and are *encouraged* in such pursuits by parents than those who are pressured into something.

When you use force, you lose power.

Consider the child who sees a relative playing a piano, then asks for guidance in fingering the keyboard. Researchers say that this child is more likely to develop talents with the piano than another child who is arbitrarily driven to a music teacher's house for expensive lessons. The same applies to other areas, including reading, sports, and scientific exploration.

One researcher, Neil Daniel of Texas Christian University in Fort Worth, sums it up this way: "Kids need to be encouraged when they're doing things right, rather than being hammered. If our research has told us anything, it's that you don't get heightened achievement from tightening the screws."

One of Daniel's assignments was to analyze the educational and family backgrounds of people who had achieved a certain high award. The overwhelmingly recurrent theme was one of parents who *inspired* rather than nagged, who set their own examples of vigorous activity, and who supported their children no matter what activities those children chose. This work has since been corroborated by even broader studies.

And the importance of letting your child choose comes out again and again. Anybody who is going to be really good at something has to be internally motivated. It requires *desire*, and we, as parents, can't *have* the desire *for* our child.

So what are some of the things you can and should do to create an environment in which your child will find things he or she desires and from which the sprouts of creativity can emerge?

A good start is to have creative materials around the house. Mozart wouldn't have created his melodies at age 3 if there hadn't been a piano in the parlor. There are a myriad of useful toys, games, and playthings available at toy stores today. Some video games are great for stimulating imagination. If you have a computer at home, the creative possibilities can be endless.

Ordinary things like paper, scissors, crayons, paints, clay, ribbons, cloths, blocks, sand, simple musical instruments, and even old clothes can be useful for stimulating your child's imagination and creativity.

Useful items are everywhere, and need not be expensive. A carpet support tube can become a cannon, telescope, or simply something to look and shout through. A large cardboard box from a new home appliance can provide many hours of amusement as a "house," "office," or "school room."

Providing the space, equipment, time, and encouragement for your child's play will ensure the development of his or her creative thinking. Children themselves are the scientists and inventors. Your job is merely to provide the laboratories, the facilities, and a research assistant—you—when they need one. Children must have the true scientist's independence to work as they please and to involve you or show you the products of their labors only as and when they see fit.

Toddlers usually welcome your participation in what they do, but parents must resist the temptation to *tell* them what to do. Their play is exploration, discovery, and experiment. If you insist on showing them what particular things are "for," demonstrating the "right" way of doing things, and answering questions almost before they are asked, creativity will be stifled. The art of joining in toddlers' play is to let them lead you.

When a child shows you his or her creative endeavor, always look for something that you can sincerely and honestly praise. Never point to or focus on anything critically.

If your child brings you a picture that's impossible to decipher, don't make a guess that may be wrong or pose a question as to what it's supposed to be. Those responses can discourage. A much better approach is to say something like this: "How nice. Tell daddy about your picture." Provide more positive reinforcement by hanging the picture on a bulletin board or wall of the house.

You can also encourage children to make up stories to go with their drawings. Or mutual storytelling can be employed. In this method, the parent is usually the one who begins telling a story, though after a few tries you can encourage the child to take the lead. Take the story as far as you wish, then stop and let the other person continue. Keep on alternating this way until one of you brings the story to an end.

Another idea for nurturing your child's creativity relates to questions. As any parent knows, there are stages when the child's questions are almost endless. During such stages, it's important to be a *learner* with your child, instead of always the *teacher*. Don't try to provide every answer or solution. Instead, as much as possible, either inspire your child to develop answers, or go to a reference book or third party and learn the answer together. Never be afraid to admit that you don't know the answer. Here's an example you can use: "That's an interesting question and I don't know the answer. Let's look it up in the book."

Focusing on nurturing creativity in young children is every bit as important as helping them in their academic development. In his book, *The Self-Concept of the Young Child*, Thomas D. Yawkey explains that creative thinking and expression should really be viewed as a "fourth basic **R**" which is just as essential as "reading, 'riting, and 'rithmetic" to young children. Clearly, he says, creative thinking and high self-esteem are closely linked.

The Older Child And Adult.
Highlights

- ✧ *Successful people, who are invariably creative, can often tap into a superconsciousness to help achieve their goals.*
- ✧ *Use solitude and deep relaxation to enhance your creativity.*
- ✧ *Mindstorming and brainstorming can also stimulate creativity.*
- ✧ *Don't overlook the creative potential of your dreams.*

Regardless of age, teenagers and adults also have the challenge of maintaining and enhancing their creativity. This is usually not difficult to do. Creativity is never permanently lost; it only becomes dormant or latent from lack of use and just needs to be reawakened.

Once our creativity is fully reawakened and primed, we can often tap into what appears to be a form of higher or "super" consciousness. This superconsciousness, while not scientifically verifiable or explainable, is sometimes referred to as coincidence, intuition, or serendipity.

Many of the greatest geniuses, and most successful people, in recorded history have acknowledged being able to turn on this superconsciousness to achieve their goals. For example, Ralph Waldo Emerson, the nature writer, and

Isaac Asimov, perhaps the greatest-ever science fiction writer, both spoke of how their writings "flowed out" onto the paper almost word perfect. Mozart and Beethoven reported the same phenomenon—their music seemed to come full-blown into their minds, and they simply sat down and transcribed it onto paper. Edison and Faraday, two of our greatest inventors, spoke of how their most significant principles came to them in their dreams. These people all developed their abilities to turn on superconsciousness, and they trusted it to guide them. Each of us has the potential to do the same.

One of the most effective means of priming the older person's creativity pump is through the use of solitude. The idea involves steps in the **autogenic conditioning** approach to visualization, as described on page 119.

First, select a quiet spot where you will be free of all disturbances and distractions. A beautiful, natural environment near a stream or the ocean, with singing birds or other natural sounds, is a great choice.

Next, get comfortable, close your eyes, and relax deeply and fully. This can be facilitated by counting down from 50 to 1, taking a full deep breath with each count. Another effective approach is to concentrate on relaxing one small part of your body at a time (e.g., the toes, foot, ankle, lower leg, and so on) until your entire body is relaxed.

Once you are completely relaxed, the trick is to remain in this solitude for 30 to 45 minutes. The first time you try it, this won't be easy. You will have to resist all kinds of urges...to change positions, to close a window, to get a drink of water. But gradually you *will* relax in each session; and with each session it becomes easier. When you have achieved this ideal state of relaxed solitude, your mind often begins to flow like a river with ideas and solutions to your challenges and situations. Chances are that you will generate more valuable thoughts and ideas than you can act on.

While it has different names and definitions, the use of

solitude in this basic manner is practiced worldwide by numerous cultures and religions. It has been used to maintain and enhance creativity for thousands of years. It's definitely a proven technique.

Two other proven ways to enhance your creativity are **mindstorming** and **brainstorming**. These are quite similar in one key and essential aspect: They involve *writing down* certain elements.

Mindstorming is done alone. Sit in quiet solitude with paper and pen and force yourself to write down as many answers as you can to some challenge, situation, or dilemma. The more answers you can write, the better. Don't wrestle with what's *doable*, just focus on what's *right* for the situation. Often the perfect answer just jumps out at you. When this happens, take immediate action to implement it. If you use this method on a regular basis, your creativity will gradually increase to the point where you generate more useful solutions during your mindstorming sessions than you have time in the day to implement.

Brainstorming is similar to mindstorming, except it involves a group. Dozens of books have been written on this topic and some of the key recurrent criteria for successful brainstorming are:

1) limit group size to about four to seven individuals;
2) limit the length of time to about 30 to 45 minutes;
3) make the question or challenge being dealt with very narrow and specific;
4) do not evaluate or judge the ideas (i.e., allow "cross-talk")—the goal is to produce as many ideas as possible in the time allotted;
5) delegate at least one member of the group as a scribe to write down the thoughts; and
6) encourage everyone's participation—for example, go around the table and ask each person to either contribute or "pass" on each "round."

A few years ago, I had a chance to find out firsthand how ignoring such brainstorming principles can totally stifle the creative process and lead to failure of the effort. At a cost of several hundred thousand dollars, my employer had gathered several hundred regional employees together to chart new agency missions and goals. Brainstorming sessions held over the course of several days were to provide the basis for developing these new directions. But the brainstorming groups were composed of 25 to 35 people, "crosstalk" was permitted, and the brainstorming topics were overly broad and vague. The result could have been predicted—creativity was stifled, not enhanced. And the new directions that emerged were the preexisting visions of a handful of the participants.

> *Nothing so much convinces me of the boundlessness of the human mind as its operations in dreaming.*

Creativity was surely stifled in this instance, but there's one place where our creativity and the superconsciousness are always at work: our dreams. Research has shown that we dream, on average, about 2 hours a night. Whether we remember them or not, we usually experience from four to seven dream sequences each night. These dreams can be a tremendous creative resource. Freud remarked that our dreams are "the royal road to the unconscious" from which basic creativity springs. The examples of people from all fields and endeavors using their dreams for decision-making and creative breakthroughs are almost limitless.

Harnessing the creative power of our dreams requires only two things: that we clearly recall the dream, and that we are open-minded as to its message. Each of us is the ultimate authority on our own dreams. The best place to start building on interpretation is with your initial "gut" reaction.

You can do several things to improve recalling your dreams. First, say to yourself as you prepare for bed, "I do remember my dreams." Second, be ready to promptly record each dream on paper or with a tape recorder. You usually have only 10 minutes after waking before the memory of the dream is gone. Third, if you awaken spontaneously from a dream, take a moment or two to visualize yourself back in the dream—this time *aware* that you're dreaming. And finally, arrange your life to awaken spontaneously rather than by an alarm if possible. The alarm disturbs your recall process.

Once you have taken command of dream recall, you can organize your dreams in a diary or journal. Add to them your related feelings and thoughts. You may want to share some of these with family or friends. The process may lead to the awakening of one of your most abundant sources of creativity and give you access to your superconsciousness.

CHAPTER 15

Dealing With Common Situations

Your road to turning your children into successful adults will never be absolutely smooth. Invariably, there will be "potholes"—or problems—along the way. As discussed earlier, and in keeping with the attitudes of winners, you need to consider these problems as challenges or situations. Let's take time now to examine some common situations and discuss briefly how they might best be handled by parents.

Discipline.
Highlights

✧ *Don't equate discipline with punishment.*

✧ *Good discipline begins with clear, realistic rules applied with quiet firmness.*

✧ *Children interpret lack of disciplining by their parents as lack of caring and love.*

✧ *Good discipline requires:*
   ✧ *consistency and a united front by both parents;*
   ✧ *providing logical consequences to your child's actions;*
   ✧ *administering discipline in private.*

✧ *Change "you" messages to "I" messages when administering discipline to keep your child from becoming
   defensive.*

Picture these common examples:

✧ A woman is shopping with her 5-year-old son, who is
   alternately whining and weeping because he wants an
   expensive toy. Finally, the mother loses all patience
   and screams, "That's it! You're going to get the biggest
   time-out you've ever had when we get home!"

✧ A 10-year-old girl is reminded to clean her room by
   the end of the weekend. As Monday rolls around, it's
   still a mess. Her exasperated mother blows up, "Fine,"
   she says. "You're not going to summer camp, young
   lady!"

✧ A 5-year-old boy wants the toy his younger sister is
   playing with, and when she resists, he hits her and
   pulls the toy away. Seeing this, the father wheels
   around, whacks the boy and snarls, "I've told you a
   hundred times, don't hit!"

> ### *Your children more attention pay
> to what you do than what you say.*

It ought to be pretty clear what's wrong in each of these
examples. In the first instance, the valuable disciplinary
method of a time-out, immediately isolating out-of-control
children to calm them down, was misapplied by displaying
hostility and delaying the action. In the case of the messy

10 year old, the punishment far outweighed the crime. And the father who hit his son was, by his own behavior, modeling what he has just told his son not to do.

"There are now so many disciplinary techniques that ought to be used that parents just don't know about," says Dr. James Windell, who wrote a book specifically to help parents learn approaches that will result in well-behaved, self-confident children. "Too many parents fail to question the methods they use until their child develops a serious problem," he goes on. Windell exposes parents to a variety of methods, so that they can use different disciplinary tactics for different situations, depending on the age and temperament of the child.

One of the foremost mistakes parents make is to equate discipline with punishment rather than guidance and instruction. Punishment is something we do *to* the child when he or she is rebellious or blatantly fails to obey. Discipline should be viewed as something the parent does *for* the child. Good discipline depends on an atmosphere of quiet firmness and clarity; bad discipline involves harsh or inappropriate punishment, often including verbal attacks and destructive criticism directed at the child.

Discipline is an essential preparation for the outside world; it invariably results in a happier and better-behaved child. Good discipline begins with clear, simple, and realistic rules, which must be appropriate for the child's age and enforced with reasonable consequences. Rules must be repeated often for toddlers. As children advance in age and independence, modify rules appropriately and explain why.

Another common parental mistake is ignoring unacceptable behavior until a breaking point has been reached. Keep in mind that children always feel better about themselves when their parents are confident enough to set and reasonably enforce rules and limits.

To illustrate, consider this picture of Becky. Her parents have always given her an abundance of freedom. Now, at age 15, she's the envy of her friends because she's become a law unto herself. She goes where she wants, does what she wants, and says what she feels like saying. Her parents view their role as providing a home and the basic comforts of life, but they exert little, if any, effective discipline.

Becky is outwardly happy about her freedom. She often boasts to her friends and even teases them about their restrictions and rigid disciplining. But inwardly, Becky is not as happy as she pretends. She interprets the lack of parental discipline as a lack of caring and thinks to herself, "Why don't they love me enough to *make* me do what I should do?"

Often, a child like Becky will resort to "testing the limits" by making her behavior more and more objectionable or deviant. It's as if he or she is asking, "How far do I have to go before my parents will stop me?" This underlying message may be felt by far more of our children than we realize. A recent national survey of graduating high school seniors found that more than 90 percent wished their parents loved them enough to have disciplined them *more*.

If you can accept that your children both *need* and *want* you to provide discipline, then what are some of the other positive guidelines that you can follow to be more effective parents? For one thing, show consistency and a united front. As I said earlier, don't undermine rules set by your spouse. Any parental disagreements over child rearing should be resolved privately and not in front of the children. And don't allow a child to play one parent against the other, as in the old "good-guy/bad-guy" routines often employed at car dealerships. Remember that inconsistency works against effective discipline more strongly than any other aspect of parent-child relationships.

Good discipline also means avoiding temptations to protect children too much from the natural consequences of their own behavior. Here's another common situation: Injo, who is 18 years old, is a sound sleeper; it has always been hard for him to get up and get himself going in the morning. Knowing this, his parents wake him—not once, but several times each morning. Now, as a college freshman, he still expects this parental service, and his parents are convinced that without their intervention he would miss his 8 o'clock class each day.

But are his parents really doing Injo a service? Although they see themselves as loving and helpful, they have assumed a responsibility for discipline that belongs to Injo. In the process, they're fostering his feelings of indolence and helplessness. They should have bought the boy a loud alarm long ago, disciplined him to get up by himself, and let *him* face any consequences from his oversleeping.

Another guideline for good discipline is to do it in private. Avoid correcting your child when others, especially friends, are around. It is demeaning to the child and self-defeating for the parent. As we learned earlier, embarrassment lowers your child's self-esteem.

Finally, the way you deliver a discipline message to your child can have a bearing on its effectiveness. Some experts believe that parents would do well to change most of their "you" messages to "I" messages as much as possible. The "you" message is all too often what we hear: "You make me mad!" or "You never clean your room without being reminded" or "You're acting like a baby."

Less friction is generated and better feelings maintained by use of "I" messages, which can deliver the same points: "I'm getting upset; I don't like feeling this angry" or "I've got more work than I can handle; I don't think I should have responsibility for your room" or "I can't handle all this crying and whining; it's making me nervous and cranky."

While "I" messages may not solve all communication problems, they can help get parents' messages across in a manner that is less likely to put the child on the defensive and generate negative emotions.

Punishment.
Highlights

- ✧ *Physically punishing your child can too easily escalate into child abuse.*

- ✧ *If you decide to use physical punishment, follow these rules:*
  - ✧ *Never administer punishment when angry;*
  - ✧ *Never strike your child in the face;*
  - ✧ *Never use punishment that leaves long-lasting marks on your child's body;*
  - ✧ *Immediately follow the punishment with assurances of your unconditional love.*

- ✧ *Replacing physical punishment with logical consequences eliminates many problems between parent and child.*

The debate over whether to punish and what kind of physical punishment is acceptable to use with a child goes on. Nevertheless, the link between *severe* physical punishment during childhood and later psychological disorders in adulthood is already well established. And more recent studies suggest that even mildly harsh punishment in childhood results in certain psychological disorders later.

For example, one research team at Washington University in St. Louis found that the majority of adult depressives and alcoholics in one group reported childhood beatings with a belt or stick, often hard enough to still feel pain or see a doctor the next day. A much smaller percentage of the "healthy" portion of the group recalled such severe treatment. Given the findings, the researchers cautioned parents, educators, and governments to beware not only of blatant child abuse but of how children's day-to-day misbehavior is handled. They noted that "many of the parental practices found to be deleterious would not qualify as gross neglect or abuse" but nevertheless leave children "with a mark in the way they are able to deal with life and cope with their problems."

Quite obviously then, parents must exercise extreme care when walking the fine line between physical punishment and child abuse. Three simple guidelines can help in this endeavor: 1) never administer *any* physical punishment when you're angry; it's just too easy for things to get out of hand and turn to abuse. 2) never under any circumstances strike the child in the face, and never administer any physical punishment, such as a spanking, for which a mark persists on the child's body after more than an hour. 3) immediately after the punishment, demonstrate your unconditional love to the child. He or she must always know that it was the behavior alone that caused the action on your part.

Parents may be better off replacing all physical punishment with natural or logical consequences. This is the approach recommended by Rudolph Dreikurs, one of America's best-known child psychiatrists, in his excellent book, *Children: The Challenge.*

Basically, the approach works like this: If Randy doesn't come home at the agreed-upon time, he misses his dinner. If Jamie forgets to take her completed homework assignment to school, she suffers whatever consequences the teacher may impose. If your 5 year old persists in running into the street, restrict him or her to playing inside the rest of the day. You can emphasize the logical consequence aspect to the child with explanations like, "When you forget and play in the street, I'm afraid a car will hit you. Play inside today, and we'll see if you can remember better tomorrow." In this manner, your action isn't perceived as punishment; it's simply the logical consequences of the child's own behavior.

For another example, let's go back for a moment to Randy, who doesn't come home on time for meals. If this becomes a real problem, you can easily follow this sequence: warn, then scold, and eventually "ground" the boy or institute some other form of appropriate punishment. But why not simply employ the logical consequence approach? The next time he's not there at mealtime, go ahead and clean up the table and put away the leftovers, if any. When Randy arrives home, tell him in a matter-of-fact way that he's welcome to get out the leftovers, provided he leaves the kitchen clean—just as he found it.

Advantages of the logical consequences approach are clear. Hostilities toward you are minimized because outcomes result directly from the child's behavior, not from the authority figure. You can remain friendly and sympathetic. You can even side with the child and express regret about the outcome. And finally, the things which could potentially damage your child's self-esteem—the inevitable adversarial roles, the shouting, the possible physical pain—can all be avoided.

> ### *You catch more flies with honey than with vinegar.*

Fear And Other Negative Emotions.
Highlights

 ✧ *Most children have anxieties and fears unique to their developmental stage.*

 ✧ *The best thing you can do to help with your children's fears is to show them how to gain more control over their environment.*

 ✧ *Another approach is to desensitize your child to a particular fear.*

 ✧ *Don't punish, tease, ridicule, or try to talk your child out of a fear.*

> ✧ *Ignore other negative expressions of emotion, but help children to "own their feelings."*
>
> ✧ *Teach children to talk about fears and express negative emotions in constructive physical activity.*
>
> ✧ *Prevent negative emotions from arising in the first place by praising the good you see in your children's actions.*

Child-care experts agree that each stage of a child's early development brings its unique set of anxieties and fears. There are certain distinct fears that the infant develops and others that show up at various ages in the toddler. Additional fears that are as unique as the child who develops them are also usually present.

During the first few months of life, babies' discomfort is mainly of a physical nature. They become distressed and cry about too much light, loud sounds, or excessive jostling.

At around 3 months of age, children generally begin to express love for mom and dad. But their newfound ability to identify the consistent providers of food, comfort, and affection has its flip side. By around 6 months of age, babies may show extreme apprehension of strangers. They will burrow their head against mom's shoulder to avoid the gaze of a newcomer. This fearfulness can even extend to people, including the caregiver, who weeks or days earlier were readily accepted.

As toddlers' sense of self-esteem grows, up through age 3, other kinds of fears emerge. During this period, they are struggling with their own individuality and the need to have some control over their lives. At the same time, they still want to feel cared for and loved by their parents. As a result of these conflicting emotions, they are vulnerable to an assortment of fears.

Some of the more common ones at this stage are aversions to insects, snakes, loud alarming sounds such as from emergency vehicle sirens, and people in unusual clothes or uniforms. The fear of animals, doctors, and bodily injuries often also develop during this period.

One child psychologist and author notes that as children get closer to the preschool years, they begin to feel more and more vulnerable. They begin to realize, perhaps through experience, that if they climb up too high and fall down, they'll get hurt.

In fact, he says, some children "temporarily develop an exaggerated fear that something is going to happen to their bodies." That may be why children this age love bandages. Maybe they feel that the Band-Aid will heal and keep them whole.

In dealing with these fears, keep in mind that you can't protect your child from all distressing experiences. While you may want a recipe for such perfection, it simply doesn't exist. You can't prevent the child from having to experience certain fears, and in many instances you shouldn't try.

Allowing Susie to remain inside because she's afraid of flies, for example, only reinforces her fear and does nothing to eliminate it. On the other hand, teasing, humiliating, or punishing her for her fears is just as destructive.

You can help most by teaching your children how to identify and master their fears. In the case of Susie's fear of flies, you can provide her with a fly swatter. If Billy is afraid to go to bed because he imagines there are monsters lurking in the shadows, give him a flashlight to keep by his pillow. An alternative might be a plastic "sword" with which to "fend them off." A child afraid of the sound of the vacuum cleaner may find relief by being allowed to turn it on and off. Each of these examples illustrates a way to give your child some degree of added control over the environment, which is a very effective means of dealing with fears.

Another approach, often used by therapists, involves gradually desensitizing the child to whatever is feared. For example, if your child is afraid of dogs, start out by drawing pictures of dogs. Then read a book about dogs. Then maybe visit a pet store or animal shelter and look at live dogs. Eventually, progress to having the child touch or pet a small dog or puppy. If need be, recognize the fear and encourage your child with words like, "It's a little scary, isn't it? Why don't we just watch for a minute, then you can give it a try."

If the fear is relatively mild, it may be best to force your child to confront it head-on. An example would be the young child who is afraid of riding in a elevator. If you ride on the elevator anyway, all the while providing whatever emotional support is needed, the fear usually subsides quickly.

Of course, fear isn't the only negative emotion your developing child will express. What do you do when the inevitable temper tantrum occurs? The best action is to deliberately ignore it. You might say to the child, "You're really upset. You need time to cool down and get yourself under control." Then simply walk out of the room and busy yourself elsewhere. Few children can maintain a tantrum without an audience.

Punishing or trying to talk the child out of it are usually poor approaches, because they're apt to intensify the emotion and teach the child that such behavior is a good way to gain attention.

Letting children "own their own feelings" is often the better approach. This concept was developed by Thomas Gordon, author of the well-known Parent Effectiveness Training (PET) Program.

Suppose your angry daughter blurts out, "I hate you!" How should you respond? Should you spank her and wash out her mouth with soap? Should you retort back, "You little brat! I hate you too!" Or should you try to *reason* away her feelings: "Honey, you *couldn't* hate your very own mother."

The best thing to do is to simply remain quiet and let the child own her emotions for the moment. Or make a nonjudgmental comment such as, "Gee, you're really mad at me aren't you?" to help her own it. In either case, the child's anger will pass quickly, and things will return to normal.

Another good method is to help your child find socially acceptable outlets for the bad feelings. If Andy is responding inappropriately when he is upset, it's up to you to guide him to more acceptable pathways. You can encourage him to talk about his feelings; this is a great tension-reliever. You can direct him toward more physical activity, involving sports or household chores. It is important that you help him find some type of emotional outlet. Repressed emotions can result in both harmful psychological and physical effects throughout childhood and on into adulthood.

Avoid punishing your child for displaying negative emotions. If and when you administer punishment, do it for bad *behavior,* not an honest expression of bad *feelings.*

Above all, however, the best way to deal with a child's emerging negative emotions is to minimize them in the first place. This is best done by always looking for the good. Find the child doing good things that please you and *tell* him or her so. A sensitive, observing parent will find countless opportunities every day for praise and nurturing statements such as these:

"I like the way you come to dinner without being reminded."
"I appreciate your hanging up your clothes even though you were in a hurry to go play."
"You were really patient while I was talking on the phone."
"Thank you for telling me the truth about what really happened."
"I'm glad you shared your candy with your sister—it's nice how you think of others."

School-Related Issues.
Highlights
⋄ *Prepare children fully for going to school and answer all questions honestly.*

✧ *Let children settle their own difficulties with schoolmates.*

✧ *Avoid emotional upset if the child obtains poor grades; focus instead on praise, encouragement, and assistance.*

✧ *Avoid predicting or rationalizing the child's poor grades; grades may only be worsened.*

✧ *Avoid making the child's homework your production.*

✧ *Help children with homework but only for brief periods when you feel calm and patient.*

1. Beginning School. One common fear that we didn't discuss in the section above deserves some special attention. This is the scariness of beginning school—either for the first time or after a long summer break.

All children go through periods of anxiety related to coming and going from the security of home and their loved ones, and starting school is certainly no exception.

One effective way to reduce school-related anxiety is to give children something special of yours to keep with them. A locket with your photo in it can be particularly reassuring to little ones who may be seeing lots of new faces for the first time. You can tape a picture of the whole family inside the lid of a child's lunch box. A piece of jewelry or small article of clothing from either parent might also do the trick. Sending Elise off to school with a little bit of "you" can go a long way towards letting her know you love her and are thinking of her, even though you aren't there in person.

Take time to fully prepare your child for beginning school to reduce anxiety. Answer all questions honestly. Tell him or her what going to school means. You can say, "When you go to school, you'll be learning and playing with a lot of other children. You'll make new friends and do lots of fun things. I'll come to your classroom soon and get to know your new friends."

Make all transportation plans clear to the child. If he or she is to walk to school, walk the route together a few times before and after school begins. You can also provide social support by arranging for your child to walk the route with other children of the same age in the neighborhood. If a bus is to be used, help your child learn to clearly identify it. You might also want to say, "I'll walk you to the bus stop the first few days, but I know you'll want to walk there alone after that, won't you?"

Treat going to school as part of the normal course of events, something that is required of your child and accepted by you. If the child is nervous, discuss his or her concerns. Show understanding and encouragement. A calm, matter-of-fact, positive attitude should be your goal.

Let your child settle any difficulties or quarrels that may arise with schoolmates. Unless children are harming each other physically, it's usually best to give them a chance to work through their own difficulties.

One final reminder: Avoid any comparisons of this child's experiences with school to how brothers, sisters, or neighbor children did. Such comparisons can be harmful to the child's self-esteem and self-image. Each of us is different, and we meet life's turning points in our own unique ways.

2. School Grades. Now that we're on the subject of school, let's talk for a moment about school grades. What should you as the parent do when your son or daughter comes home from school with a report card full of low grades? Getting upset and angry will most likely only make matters worse, according to a recent study by Stanford University researchers.

"Emotional upset is the worst possible reaction to poor grades," said the study's Director, Sanford M. Dornbusch, a human biology and sociology professor at Stanford. "When the parents become upset and the child is upset, we find an association with poor grades. Over time, grades tend to get even worse." Dornbusch also reports that parents' schemes to reward for good grades and punish for bad ones also usually lead to *lower* grades. In both instances, students become more concerned with the reward or punishment than with truly studying and learning a subject. And if grades do improve, it may be in part because Jimmy is sticking to easier or "safer" subjects, where he knows he can excel, please his parents, and claim a reward. It has a negative impact on both his curiosity and willingness to take risks.

So how should you proceed when bad grades arrive? Most experts believe the low-key use of praise, encouragement, and offers of assistance are ideal. Study results also show benefits to parents fostering independence and questioning—that is, risk-taking—in their children. Taking an active interest also seems to help. Students from families who participate in school functions tend to have better grades.

And by all means, if you can attend a conference at school regarding your child's grades, do so. This may seem simplistic, but by attending such a conference, you demonstrate your belief that school and grades are truly important. In any conference or confrontation about grades, remain positive. If your child is present, be especially careful about what you say and how you say it. Avoid any put downs or predictions of further failure as they may become self-fulfilling prophecies.

Let's say the topic of the conference is your daughter's "D" in math. Avoid saying anything negative, such as, "I was always terrible at math. Jessica's going to be the same way, I can tell." Otherwise, Jessica's next math grade may be an "F." Negative predictions by parents are all too often interpreted by children as commands to be carried out. This is one form of your child's loyalty that you want to avoid.

Here are three more interesting research findings to consider about school grades. First, a number of studies show that grades go up if a language other than English is spoken in the home. This applies to Asians, Hispanics, and foreign-born Blacks and Anglos. Second, grades are lower for the heaviest TV watchers. And third, sports participation equates with better grades, except for males who participate in organized sports more than 30 hours a week.

3. Helping With Homework. Mrs. McGraw is a caring mother who likes to be sure her children are doing their homework promptly and correctly. Recently, her son Michael was assigned by his English teacher to write an original poem. When Michael mentioned the assignment to her, Mrs. McGraw took charge. She decided what the poem would be about and helped to write each line. Michael's teacher was impressed. But how did Michael feel about the effort? Instead of feeling proud and elated, he felt uneasiness and guilt. He knew that the poem was much more his mother's creative effort than his own. His mother's actions actually showed her lack of faith in his abilities, and knowing that lowered Michael's feelings of capability and self-esteem.

This little story demonstrates an important guideline. It is generally appropriate to help and guide your child when he or she needs it. But be careful to avoid (a) assuming responsibility for the homework and (b) making it your own rather than your child's production.

Another guideline is to provide homework help only when you are calm and feeling patient. If you find yourself getting impatient or edgy, withdraw from the effort and let someone else help. Keep periods of instructional help short— less than an hour in most cases. This may be difficult, because sometimes your child will display feigned inadequacy just to gain your sympathy and keep you involved.

Duties, Chores, And The Use Of Rewards.
Highlights

  ✧ *Use reward systems involving charts and stickers or other treats on a limited basis for younger children to get them to initially perform specific tasks.*

✧ *Give any rewards with eye contact, touching, and nurturing statements.*

✧ *To get adolescents and teens to comply, clearly define the task or chore, set a time frame for completion, and use logical consequences instead of punishment for failure to comply.*

Even the best of parents who rigidly adhere to the guidance in this book may occasionally have difficulty getting their child to perform a particular task. When this occurs with the adolescent or teenager, reassess the situation to be sure that you're following two important guidelines. First, have you clearly defined the duty or chore and set a distinct starting and ending time for its completion? Here's the kind of specificity needed: "Adam, I want you to mow the grass Saturday between noon and 6 o'clock, after it has dried thoroughly enough from the morning dew" or "Rachel, you'll have to clean your room before going skating at 3 o'clock with Mary." If negotiations are needed to establish an alternate time frame, that's fine. But be sure that a distinct timetable is established at the onset.

Second, try to employ the use of "logical consequences" instead of the threat of punishment if the child fails to perform the duty or chore. If necessary, go back now and reread about logical consequences on pages 171-172 and then adapt this concept to the particular situation in which you're having trouble with your child.

To get a younger child to comply with assigned chores, you may want to try a system involving "rewards" in the form of star charts, stickers, gifts, or other treats. It's best to keep these simple. Try working on just a few behaviors at a time. Otherwise, the child may feel overwhelmed, thereby dooming the effort. To avoid singling out a particular child, try a chart for all the children, or even the whole family, with different activities and tasks appropriate to each person.

With young children, stickers or stars can be used to

indicate the completion of a job each day. Older children usually respond better to something such as check marks that they fill in after they complete a task. At the end of a prescribed period of time, perhaps a week, provide a "payoff." The reward can be an object or something immaterial, like extra time with mom or dad. Some families decide that when everyone fills in their spaces on the chart, they have a fun family activity, for instance, a trip to the zoo, horseback riding, or bowling.

Caution should be exercised with reward approaches, however. Child-rearing professionals have debated this topic for years, and the benefits and detriments are still not clearcut. The main issue can be simply put: Do rewards motivate children to do something for the sake of doing it, or do they get children to do something only because they seek the reward?

Most professionals tend to agree that reward systems can be effective under limited circumstances. The positive feedback from earning a reward lets children know what they need to do to gain your approval, which is something they want more than anything else. If the reward is also coupled with eye contact, touching, smiles, a warm tone of voice, and an approving statement, it becomes a symbol for your love and caring. Then, when you are not present, what stays with them is that positive feeling they felt when the reward was given. It is this kind of energy—not the reward itself—that has power to shape behavior without adverse consequences.

When you don't combine the energy of love with the reward, or when you give the reward grudgingly, you run the risk of the reward becoming a bribe. Giving children a payoff for something they shouldn't be doing is also a bribe. Such bribing *is* an inappropriate parenting technique because it teaches children to manipulate their behavior to receive the bribes. This in turn makes it much more difficult to instill in them basic success-achieving principles and knowledge.

Noted child psychiatrist Stanley Turecki recommends using rewards only as a jump-start. "If you have an entrenched situation with endless confrontations, stars or stickers on a temporary basis can initiate change," he says. But the reward should be dropped as quickly as possible. "Your praise and the child's sense of accomplishment need to take over," he goes on.

Star charts or similar reward systems should never be used for getting children over developmental or physical hurdles, such as toilet training, bed-wetting, or thumb sucking. And reward systems are generally useless for toddlers. Telling a 3 year old she'll get a star each day she goes without an accident and a gift after each five stars is unrealistic and a form of badgering. It won't work because the child lacks the basic skills and maturation to do what you want. Resentment toward the parent is the most likely outcome.

A better approach is a spontaneous reward given when your child has a success: "Wow! You did such a good job. You knew just when you needed to get to the bathroom. I'm so proud of you! How about a trip to the playground?"

As you move away from concrete rewards for preschoolers to more symbolic rewards for school-age children, remember to identify and acknowledge *feelings*. The approach needed is: "You should feel good about what you did. Do you?" A similar message would be: "Were you happy with what you did? Did it make you feel good inside?"

Here are a couple of final thoughts regarding the use of a star or chart system for rewarding. First, if you institute one and it isn't working, give it up. Explain to your child, "This isn't helping. We need to do something different." Second, remember that rewards should be like our goals— neither too easy nor too hard to achieve. They should make the child stretch a little without being unrealistically difficult.

The Security Blanket.
Highlights

> ❖ *Most children become attached to some cuddly thing between the ages of 1 and 2.*
>
> ❖ *Such attachments are a normal step in gaining independence from their parents.*

While packing for the family's move to his new job in another state, Roger came across Bo-Bo, his 6-year-old son Christopher's tattered teddy bear. At first, Roger tossed the toy into a pile for the Salvation Army. But later, with a twinge of sentimentality, he retrieved it and packed it with the other toys for shipping.

Shortly after arriving at their new home, Chris asked for Bo-Bo and for the next few weeks rarely let go of him. After Chris had adjusted to his new surroundings and school, the bear was relegated to the bottom of the toy box. "To think I almost threw Bo-Bo out," Roger said. "He helped Chris get through a very stressful time."

Chris' Bo-Bo and any number of other cuddly or lovable things that children become attached to are often called "security blankets" or "transitional objects."

One recent study found that stuffed animals were security blankets for 40 percent of children, while 33 percent chose blankets. Other favorites were dolls, diapers, scraps of material, and towels. Children also latched onto more unusual items such as pot holders, toothbrushes, key chains, music boxes, and even mommy's silk nightgown.

Not every infant or toddler chooses a security blanket, and experts say whether they do or not shouldn't be viewed as a problem. However, most children select something when they are between 12 and 18 months old. Typically, their love affair with the object lasts 3 or 4 years. By age 6 or 7 they lose interest in the item and turn to social activities.

Security blankets are also called transitional objects

because they help children move from the perception of being merged with their mothers to a view of themselves as independent people. A youngster's attachment to a special object is evidence of his or her relationship to the world. The object is the first thing in the world that, unlike a fist or thumb, *belongs* to the infant and yet is not a part of the infant.

Parents should refrain from worrying about, or being embarrassed by, the child who drags around some raggedy old object. A security blanket is not a childish crutch nor does it signify that the child is insecure. Such well-worn objects lead the way for the child's psychological growth and maturity. If parents feel the need to impose some restrictions on the child's use of such an object, they must be gentle. Above all, avoid any teasing or ridicule. Say something like "We don't want Smokey to catch a cold outside" or "Now that you're getting so big, it would be best if Blankie stays with you only at bedtime."

Children often demand their object when they're tired. A security blanket promotes sleep and can become an integral part of the bedtime ritual. By concentrating on this object and all the good feelings associated with it, the child can wind down from the busy activities of the day.

Other Related Situations.
Highlights

- ❖ *To cope with bed-wetting, share affirmative self-talk and don't rush the child to bed.*

- ❖ *Show encouragement but let children solve problems with other children on their own.*

- ❖ *Steer an unpopular child into social activities, encourage more at-home play, or enlist the teacher's help.*

- ❖ *Give an obese child emotional support and encouragement, not scolding or ridicule.*

✧ *Imaginary "illnesses" are a normal part of growing up.*

✧ *Try a novel approach with sibling rivalry; encourage one to do something good for the other.*

✧ *Don't subject your child's choice of friends to your approval.*

✧ *Explain divorce to children early in the process, assure them they are still loved and that it isn't their fault, and keep parent-child communication alive.*

✧ *Don't try to choose your child's vocation.*

✧ *An allowance with freedom to spend it as they wish teaches children how to make decisions involving money.*

✧ *Keep communication—not just talk—going during the teenage years.*

There are hundreds of related situations that we could deal with here, but that would be well beyond the scope or intent of this book. Here are just a few more of the common situations parents have to deal with and some suggested actions:

1. Bed-wetting. When bed-wetting is a problem, two relatively simple things may help. First, don't suddenly force the child to go to bed. Give him or her plenty of time to "wind down." You may begin by saying, "Okay, now, it's bedtime. You have 20 minutes to finish coloring, put on your pajamas, and go to the bathroom." Second, share affirmative self-talk with the child as you're tucking him or her in. Something like "You always sleep in a warm, dry bed and if you need to go to the bathroom, you always give me or your daddy a call" can be very effective.

2. Problems With A Bully. When your child is being bothered by a bully, you may be tempted to step in and resolve the situation. However, as mentioned earlier, this is usually a mistake. The bully may make things even more miserable for your child. And if both parents get involved, they usually only see their child's side of the story and can't deal objectively with the situation. It's much better to let your child solve the problem.

You can encourage your child to stand up to the bullying. Bullies usually pick on others out of their own feelings of inferiority and weakness. They assume that those they attack will run away, avoid them, or not fight back. When they find this not to be the case, they often back down.

Special consideration is needed, however, for bullies who are severely maladjusted, sadistic, or even psychotic. In cases like this, parents may need to take the issue to the bully's parent, a school official, or even a law enforcement officer.

3. Unpopularity. The child who is unpopular may need some special considerations. Why are some children unpopular? It may simply be the nature of the child or a question of how much exposure the child has had to other youngsters at an early age. Unpopularity may also be the result of physical differences, such as a big nose or different clothing. Less obvious causes are differences in hearing, vision, or speech. Your child may also be driving other children away with selfishness, bossiness, or bullying behavior.

Many experts believe that unpopularity in children is often a direct result of lack of early parental involvement and leaving too much of the child-rearing to teachers and the community. But it's never too late to begin to correct this situation.

Start by showing concern and empathy, as well as letting your child know that it isn't a failing to not have lots of friends. "One good friend can be enough. This is not unusual at all," you might say. Also, reassure your child that it's okay to be exactly *who* he or she is. At the same time, if the child's behavior appears to be the root of the problem, point it out.

You can also steer your child into social activities with other children. Examples include preschool, baby-sitting co-ops, or later, such groups as Cub Scouts, Girl Scouts and church activities. Encourage "at-home play times" by providing safe and attractive things that other children enjoy. The home with enticing play equipment or some special toys will draw other children. You can also enlist the help of other parents by inviting them to bring a child to play. One visitor at a time may be best; otherwise it's too easy for the situation to become the visitors against one.

Parents of an unpopular child may also need to enlist the teacher's help. An informed teacher can easily go to bat for the child. One tactic might be to hold a class meeting and get the students thinking about others with such questions as "How would *you* feel if...?" (be exact) or "How do *you* think someone would feel if...?" (be exact). This approach can be highly effective, since most children don't intend to be mean or hurtful. They just don't realize they're doing so.

4. Obesity. The obese child needs positive emotional support, not scolding or ridicule. Also, avoid constantly talking about weight problems around the child. Maggie already knows she's "fat" and doesn't need to be reminded. Encouragement and positive reinforcement for sticking to low-calorie foods is much more effective than destructive criticism or scolding.

Parents should also be aware that overeating can be a sign of emotional stress in the child. The child may be tense or worried about something. Or the problem may be even more serious—substituting food for feelings of love and acceptance that the parents are not providing.

Remember, also, that obesity is not only the result of overeating or lack of self-discipline. There are often distinct hereditary factors, too. For example, in one study adopted children were found to compare more closely to their natural parents in body type than to their adoptive parents and more closely to their natural siblings than to the siblings they grew up with. In another study, identical twins were fed 1,000 calories over their normal intake a day. Weight gain varied from 9 to 29 pounds, but predictably, twins were closer in weight gain to each other than to non-siblings.

5. Imaginary Illnesses. Imaginary illnesses may, at times, develop in children. The "illness" may be the result of a test or some function at school that they're afraid of. If you let them cop out, you're training them to do the same thing later in life. Insist that they participate and try their best. Such stressful junctures are just a normal part of growing up.

6. Sibling Fights. When sibling fights get out of hand, various approaches may be needed, but here's one simple scenario worth trying. Let's say that Robert and Robin have had a serious falling out with each other. Robert says he wants to go to Robin's room and take or break something. You talk calmly with Robert, letting him vent as much steam as possible. Then you suggest that, instead of following his natural inclinations, he do something nice for his "enemy." It may not be easy to convince him at first, but if you persist and are successful, the benefits can be astonishing. Both you and Robert can enjoy Robin's befuddlement as she tries to figure out her benefactor. And the act should lead to everyone having better feelings.

7. Children's Friends. Generally, a child's friends should not be subjected to parental approval. Admittedly, it may be difficult for you to stand by and watch your child form alliances with others whose appearances, traits, or behaviors you dislike. But after children reach a certain age, parents have little ability to significantly influence their choice of friendships. And your efforts to do so are apt to be met with resistance and defiance. In fact, if a child is ever going to feel the need to rebel against parental authority, this is one area where it is likely to surface.

Your best bet is to rely on the good set of values you've already taught them. In the long run, the confidence you show in your children's judgment and ability to choose their friends will strengthen your relationship with them and raise their self-esteem.

8. Minimizing Divorce Effects. To minimize effects of divorce on the child, pay attention to at least three key areas. First, parents need to explain the divorce to their children in an age-appropriate way. Experts agree that it's best to tell them as soon as the decision has been made. Only a foolish parent would think that the emotional upheaval associated with a divorce can be hidden from a child—even a very young child.

Second, parents must assure children that the divorce is not their fault and that they are still loved by *both* parents. Children commonly blame themselves for parental breakups and then torture themselves—perhaps for years—wondering what they could have done to prevent it.

Third, try to keep communications going. Parents may want to limit the talk of separation, but the more said, the better. Bringing the children into the discussions and letting them express their feelings before, during, and after the divorce can be good for everyone's emotional health.

9. Vocational Choice. The child's vocation should be something that evolves from the child. Savvy parents know that it is best not to pressure a child into following in their footsteps. If parents are successful, happy, and enthusiastic about their professions, there's every chance that a son or daughter will want to have the same kind of job, but it should never be expected. Nor should parents expect children to live their *unfulfilled* vocational dreams: "Son, dad had to drop out of law school to support grandma and your aunts, but you'll be able to attend."

10. Allowances. An allowance for children is an idea that is embraced by most child-rearing experts. Age 7 or 8 is usually a good time to begin. Give a modest amount at first and increase it as children get older. Don't give a child extra money if he or she runs short.

Children should be given considerable freedom in how they spend their allowance. But parents can encourage them to save a portion for some worthwhile purpose. Whatever mistakes children make in spending their allowance should be considered lessons learned for the future when the stakes will be much higher.

To help children learn even more financial lessons for the future, it may also be a good idea to involve them in the family's finances. For example, let them shop for the groceries, prepare checks for your signature to pay bills, or even plan the household budget. Teenagers who understand how the family's funds are being spent will be less likely to make unreasonable demands on family coffers.

11. Teenage Years. Those terrible teenage years is a subject on which entire books have been written, and I can't begin to do the subject justice here. But let me offer this one piece of advice: Keep the *communication*—not just talk—going between you and the teenager. Parents often find it difficult to really communicate at this stage. Fortunately, if the relationship has been good until now, and you've taught him or her solid principles, any communication gaps are likely to be only temporary.

Parents need to remember that, more than at any other stage, the teen years are when children most seek and want the acceptance and friendship of peers. That's why it is at this age that they are most likely to deviate from previous standards of behavior as they seek such acceptance.

PART FOUR:

Maintaining Wellness

In this concluding part of the book I want to discuss the issue of maintaining wellness. This is another subject about which whole books are written. But there are four key aspects of this topic that seem to be more important—and affect the success of more people—than all other aspects of wellness combined. These are: 1) weight control and dieting; 2) exercise; 3) smoking; and 4) stress reduction.

CHAPTER 16

Weight Control and Dieting

Highlights

✧ *Being overweight puts us at a greater risk for such serious diseases as heart malfunction, hypertension, diabetes, and possibly cancer.*

✧ *Rigid dieting triggers the body's caloric deprivation response, which increases fat storage efficiency and lowers the metabolic rate.*

✧ *A regimen of prudent eating is much more effective; for adults, this means:*
   ✧ *don't skimp on breakfast;*
   ✧ *don't make the evening meal the largest of the day;*
   ✧ *avoid fast foods and other fat-laden foods;*
   ✧ *eat slower to eat less;*
   ✧ *stick to wholesome foods rather than fatty, highly processed ones.*

✧ *An ideal rate of weight loss is ½ to 1 pound a week.*

✧ *Strict dieting for children is not advised.*

✧ *Both calorie and vitamin needs go up when a woman is pregnant; her diet should increase by 300 to 400 calories a day with care taken to ensure all vitamin needs are met.*

Here's the United States' bulge divulged: Ohio and Wisconsin are the states with the highest percentages of overweight people; the states of Hawaii and New Mexico have the lowest percentages of overweight residents. Across the U.S., about 22 percent of all men and 21 percent of all women tip the scales on the high side, for a whopping total of 34 million overweight Americans. For older Americans, the statistics are even grimmer. For example, roughly a third of U.S. residents over the age of 50 are overweight.

> ## *Those who ignore health in the pursuit of wealth usually lose both.*

Statistics from the Federal Centers for Disease Control show that people who are overweight put themselves at greater risk for serious diseases, including diabetes, heart disease, hypertension, and possibly cancer. Poor diet and low activity combine as the Number 2 killer of people in the U.S., ranking just behind smoking as an actual cause of death. And as we've learned earlier in this book, there are a multitude of behavioral side effects from being obese. Overweight people may be ridiculed and made the brunt of hurtful jokes. Their jobs or schooling may suffer. And their feelings of self-esteem and self-image may be seriously eroded.

It's no wonder that the dieting industry has become one of America's biggest businesses. This is despite the fact that more than 90 percent of all dieters *regain* all the weight they've lost within 3 years, and about half grow to an even greater weight than before.

The so-called "crash" or all-liquid diets are probably the worst. This is what TV talk-show host Oprah Winfrey used the first time she trimmed down to svelte proportions about 4 years ago.

Such diets are almost always doomed to failure because of the body's own built-in defense mechanisms. What happens is this: When we reduce our calories to the point of hunger and weakness, the body responds by increasing the production and biological activity of a fat-storage enzyme called lipoprotein lipase. When we go off the diet, this enzyme continues its overactivity. It causes fat to build up *again*, this time with such efficiency that all too soon we may be carrying around more than we originally had. That's right! We often actually *increase* our body fat as a direct result of dieting.

Dieting also slows down our resting metabolic rate, so it becomes harder for our bodies to burn off calories. The latest research out of the Oregon Health Sciences University in Portland shows that this reduced metabolic rate can persist for 2 months following a diet of the same duration. During that period alone, the reduced metabolic rate could cause you to put back all the fat you have lost and then some. Couple this with the lipoprotein lipase effect described above, and a stringent 2-month-long diet could result in your being 5 pounds heavier than before. Engage in such destructive behavior for 10 years, and you can find yourself with 50 pounds of excess blubber. The point is, to have the body of a winner, we need to avoid dieting and never consider going on a crash diet. Either approach is counter-productive.

> *A stringent diet can put on 5 pounds.*
> *Do this every year for 10 years*
> *and you'll be 50 pounds fatter.*

These are not the only reasons to avoid dieting. Another good reason is that cutting calories may seriously cut your body's ability to fight diseases and infections. In a study at the University of Tsukuba in Japan, athletes on low-calorie diets experienced between 11 and 18 percent declines in the activity of two types of white blood cells involved in immune-system responses. This occurred despite the subjects taking vitamin supplements during the diets.

Another problem with dieting pertains to teens. Today's "thin is in" philosophy keeps teenage girls in particular from getting all the calcium they need when they need it most according to a recent Ohio State University study. Adequate calcium is crucial for teenagers. Almost half of the adult skeleton is built during adolescence when bodies are most efficient at absorbing calcium. But the Ohio State study found that only 16 percent of the subjects, girls ranging in age from 11 to 18, met today's 1,200 mg daily recommended intake for calcium.

Researchers from both Ohio State University and the Mayo Clinic concluded that getting adequate calcium during the growth years may be the best prevention for crippling osteoporosis later in life. The smaller the peak bone mass or total amount of bone present up to age 3, the greater the risk of osteoporosis later on. A recent National Institutes of Health study found that a little extra daily calcium, about the amount in a cup of skim milk, boosted adolescent girls' (aged 12 to 14) bone-building rate by 20 percent. Those most in need of calcium supplementation are weight-conscious teens, who often seek out "fast foods" that are high in fats and low in calcium. For these same girls, carbonated drinks—especially colas—often become the drink of choice in preference to natural juices or milk which is high in calcium but perceived as fattening.

One particularly nasty ingredient in the colas that are so popular with our children is phosphoric acid. Colas often have 35 to 40 mg of this ingredient, which in turn tends to "pull" the phosphorus and magnesium out of the body. Magnesium is essential for regulating blood pressure, and a deficiency of magnesium in the teen years may set the stage for heart disease in later life.

Carbonated cola drinks can also further damage an aging woman's bones at a time when estrogen levels and bone mass normally decline. A recent Harvard University study of several thousand women graduates ranging in age from 21 to 80, many of whom were athletic in college, revealed that their risk of bone fractures more than doubled if they habitually drank nonalcoholic carbonated beverages. The women in the study drank between 16 and 23 ounces of soft drinks a day, and fracture risk rose with greater consumption. However, the researchers were unable to gauge a "safe" limit. While the cause of the link between soda drinking and higher risk for fractures isn't known, phosphoric acid is at least a strong suspect.

The detriments of soda drinking could be affecting a significant proportion of aging women. Overall, the per capita soda consumption in the U.S. has tripled over the past 30 years.

So if adults and teenagers need to avoid excess soft drink consumption and dieting, what about our children? Strict dieting to reduce weight is almost never advisable for children who are still growing, even if they're fat. Check with your doctor, of course, if in doubt about your child's health in relation to obesity. But generally, the most desirable approach is a combination of exercise and *prudent eating*. An obese child may be better off maintaining weight as he or she grows rather than trying to lose any significant amount.

Prudent eating, whether applied to the obese child, teenager, or adult, doesn't mean skimping on breakfast. Not only is a good breakfast essential for growing children, it makes no sense at all for the older adult to skip it as part of any weight control effort. The calories taken in at breakfast are actually burned more effectively by the body than calories taken in later in the day. Skipping breakfast may also lead to more snacking on high-fat, high-calorie treats later in the day.

A study by doctors at Memorial Hospital of Newfoundland, Canada, has found that skipping breakfast also impacts the blood's clotting potential. When the test subjects skipped breakfast, blood platelet "stickiness" averaged 2.5 times greater than when breakfast was eaten. According to the researchers, these findings suggest that forgoing breakfast might boost the risk of morning heart attacks.

Prudent eating also means that we eat slower in order to eat less. Have you ever wondered why you felt so uncomfortably full 30 minutes after wolfing down a big meal when you still felt hungry right afterwards?

The 20-minute satiety (fullness) principle is at work here. You may have heard that it takes about 20 minutes for the brain to register satiety, but you've probably never thought of applying this principle to your own nutrition. It's easy. Just eat slower, taking time to chew and enjoy your food. You might even try putting your utensils down after every bite or two.

Also make a point of eating the low-fat foods first. By the time you get to the higher-fat foods, you'll have started to feel satiated, so you'll be less inclined to overindulge.

Another aspect of *prudent eating* is that we don't make our evening meal the largest meal of the day, and we don't consume this meal or any snacks during the 3 to 4 hours before bedtime. Doing so is a sure route to eventual weight gain, because excess calories taken in late in the day are more likely to be converted to fat stores.

If we're adults, *prudent eating* means that we do try to eat as little fat as possible. We should certainly keep our fat intake under 30 percent of our total daily caloric intake; 20 to 25 percent is even better. The problem is that fat provides a lot of calories—9 per gram, to be exact. The carbohydrates and protein that we consume both provide less than half of this amount—about 4 calories per gram.

In the face of a massive education effort in the U.S. over the past 10 to 20 years, most of us know which of our foods are higher in fat. Butter, whole milk, egg yolks, salad dressings, potato chips, cakes, cookies, and ice cream are among the most obvious offenders. But very high fat content often occurs in unsuspected foods, too, so always take the time to read the nutritional label. And be especially cautious of so-called "fat-free" foods. The Food and Drug Administration allows ½ gram of fat *per serving* in any product that is labeled fat-free. What if the serving size is quite small— say 1 tablespoon—as is true with many nonfat salad dressings? How often do you use a tablespoon to measure your salad dressing? The point is that you can get a lot of calories, and even lots of fat, from so-called nonfat foods.

> ## *A waist is a terrible thing to mind.*

Avoiding fats and *eating prudently* also means that we need to avoid the easiest places to eat, those fast-food restaurants that jam every intersection and line busy roads. For a few years, the fast-food chains made big strides towards fat reduction in their menus, but the trend seems to be reversing itself. Just consider a few of today's breakfast menu items from the major chains: An Egg McMuffin is probably among the "leanest" with a whopping 37 percent fat (and about 290 calories). A Great Danish and Croissan'wich with sausage each contains over 500 calories, with more than two-thirds from fat.

And if that's not bad enough, fast foods are also often incredibly high in sodium. For example, eat another chain's Crescent with sausage for breakfast and you're blasted with 1,289 mg of sodium. This is pretty close to the lower range recommended for sodium intake for the entire day by the American Heart Association.

For kids, avoidance of fast-food joints and high-fat foods doesn't appear as necessary. In fact, strict low-fat diets can be outright dangerous during the child's first 2 years of life by interfering with normal growth. Such diets should never be started for children without consulting a physician or registered dietitian. After 2 years of age, moderately low-fat diets may be okay. The main thing is to be sure school-age children are getting a balanced, high-nutrient array of foods. The "30 percent of fats" rule should pretty much be ignored. In one study, researchers discovered that those children who consumed less than 30 percent of total calories from fat also failed more than half the time to get the minimum recommended daily allowances for vitamins B-12, E, thiamin, and niacin.

Our basic goal as adults and parents should be to provide a healthy, nutritious diet that makes us lean and keeps us that way, is filling and satisfying, and avoids too many calories. Do such diets exist? Yes, a number of books and studies show that they do.

Most fast foods are fat foods.

Here's some basic eating guidance that is central to many of today's best books: Put your *focus* on **wholesome foods**— fruits, hot cereals, skim milk, soups, salads, fish, chicken, turkey, rice, vegetables, and whole-grain breads and rolls. Remove the skin from chicken and turkey either before or after cooking, and you'll reduce the fat content even further. *Avoid* diets leaning towards the **fatty/refined foods,** such as bacon, eggs, buttered toast, fast foods, fried foods, roast or steak, buttered vegetables, whole milk, cakes, and ice cream.

In a recent study conducted by the University of Alabama, wholesome-food eaters achieved full satisfaction from as little as 1,500 calories a day, whereas those consuming the fatty/refined products needed 3,000 calories to be satisfied.

On a diet of wholesome foods, with a particular emphasis on reduction of fats, adults can expect to see any excess weight *slowly* begin to melt away. This is the ideal situation. The best rate of weight loss is estimated to be about ½ to 1 pound a week. If you take weight off slowly this way, you're more likely to keep it off, because the slow rate usually fools the body so that it fails to trigger its natural defense mechanisms.

The one time we shouldn't be concerned with trying to fool the body's defense mechanisms is during pregnancy. A pregnant woman must focus clearly on proper weight *gain*. She should increase her caloric intake to gain weight for herself and the child. Physicians generally suggest a total gain of between 25 and 30 pounds.

The recommended daily caloric allowance for women of childbearing age is about 2,000 calories, plus about 300 to 400 more a day during pregnancy. If the mother exercises, she'll need to up her calories, depending on the type and duration of exercise. Increasing carbohydrates in her diet is particularly important; she needs the added carbs both for her exercise and her developing baby's growth needs.

All vitamin needs also increase during pregnancy. One vitamin of particular importance is folic acid, part of the B-complex group. The requirement for this vitamin doubles during pregnancy, and recent research shows that, if taken before or very early in pregnancy, it greatly reduces chances of the baby being born with neural tube defect (which can damage the spinal cord and brain). Folic acid is found in such foods as green leafy vegetables, asparagus, and liver, but it can be difficult to obtain adequate amounts through foods alone. That's why the American Academy of Pediatrics has advocated fortifying foods with this essential B vitamin. As with any supplements being considered during pregnancy, always consult with your physician first, however.

CHAPTER 17

Exercise

Highlights

✧ *Most adults require regular exercise in addition to prudent eating for long-term weight control.*

✧ *To gain the most benefit from exercise, plan three or four aerobic (60 to 80 percent of maximum heart rate) exercise sessions a week at least 20 to 30 minutes long.*

✧ *Slow and steady exercise burns the most fat.*

✧ *Walking at a rate of 4 miles per hour is a great way to burn fat.*

✧ *The most effective times for exercise are first thing in the morning and just before dinner.*

✧ *Barely half the children in the U.S. get at least the minimum amount of regular exercise necessary to maintain healthy bodies.*

✧ *Regular exercise improves school performance and other mental activities.*

Effective weight control involves a double-edged sword, and *exercise* is the other "edge" that works together with *prudent eating*. It's close to impossible to keep weight off without exercise. A recent survey published in a major nutrition journal showed that 90 percent of the people who were successful at weight reduction exercised regularly.

> *Most poor health in the country may be attributed to heavy meals and light work.*

Regular exercise also triggers a host of other benefits. For example, the blood's level of high-density lipoprotein (HDL), the so-called "good" cholesterol, is raised, and this helps protect against heart disease. Blood pressure can be lowered, sometimes alleviating the need for medication (of course, check with your doctor first). The risk factor for adult-onset diabetes is significantly lessened—by one-quarter to one-third—with exercise.

The risk of colon cancer can be cut in half, apparently because food moves more rapidly through the digestive system, giving carcinogens less contact with colon linings. The risk of getting arthritis can also be reduced by exercise. And for people that do have it, exercise can increase the range of motion, while reducing pain in the affected joints.

And regular exercise is essential for women (along with plenty of calcium) to prevent that dreaded bone-thinning disease—osteoporosis—from affecting the spine and other major bones.

Aerobic exercise (that for which metabolic processes involving oxygen are used) forces the body to improve its ability to use oxygen, which in turn benefits the heart and lungs. Just about any level of aerobic intensity can be beneficial, but you do the most good when exercising at around 60 to 80 percent of your maximum heart rate for at least three 20 to 30 minute sessions a week. You can estimate your maximum heart rate by subtracting your age from 220. At age 40, for example, your maximum heart rate is 180, and your "target" aerobic exercise rate is about 108 to 144 beats per minute.

Starting an aerobic exercise program for the first time, or getting back into one after a hiatus, is often troublesome. People too often believe that they can reverse all the damage done with just a few weeks of exercise; that view is unrealistic if their bodies have been subjected to many years of too little exercise and poor diet.

Make your goal to get back into a "rhythm" in which exercise is a regular part of your daily schedule and life. Be willing to give something else up if need be to make time for exercise. Start gradually and set realistic goals. Exercising too much too soon after months or even years of inactivity often results in physical injuries which can set you back. A gradual, moderate return to physical activity is the prudent approach that minimizes risk of injury. People over 50 in particular should consult a physician before embarking on a program of regular physical activity.

Sudden death while exercising is an extremely rare event even among older participants. Ample studies demonstrate this. Nevertheless, watch for warning signs that may indicate serious problems or susceptibility to injury. These include pain or a "funny feeling" in the chest, nausea or abdominal discomfort, dizziness, light-headedness, or just overall fatigue. Always heed such messages from your body; they indicate a need to slow down, rest, or possibly see a doctor.

It's also important to choose an aerobic activity that you really enjoy. One of the main reasons people don't stick with aerobic programs is that they don't enjoy them. Rather than switching to something else that they might enjoy, they often give up altogether.

The key to using aerobic exercise to condition the cardio-respiratory system and control weight by burning fat is to go slowly but steadily. This is what really stokes up the body's fat-burning furnace. Short bursts of energy, such as in running sprints, increase storage of glycogen and the ability of the body to draw upon these energy stores. But longer, endurance-type activity is what really increases the body's ability to burn fat for energy. The body is stimulated to increase the number and density of mitochondria, the so-called "energy factories," in the cells.

During the first 3 to 5 minutes of exercise, the body primarily metabolizes carbohydrates. After several minutes, depending on the individual and exercise intensity, the body switches over to drawing on fat stores. And here's the neat part: The lower the intensity, the better the warm-up, and the more gradually you pick up the intensity, the quicker you'll *shift* over to this fat-burning mode. The better shape your aerobic system is in, the more total fat you'll burn. In other words, each of us has the ability to *train* our aerobic system to burn off fat more efficiently.

One of the best "fat trainers" is walking. Emphasizing this in his best-selling book, *Fit or Fat?*, Covert Bailey says that if he were grossly fat, he would give up whatever necessary—job, housework, whatever—and would walk 3 to 4 hours per day.

Clearly, however, that amount of walking is a bit extreme and unnecessary for most people. An average-sized person burns about 150 calories by walking for just 30 minutes; this, combined with reducing your diet by 150 calories a day (*easily* done just by watching your intake of fats), works out to two-thirds of a pound of weight lost per week—an almost perfect reduction regime.

While walking can be one of the best aerobic exercises, some consideration needs to be given to speed. Most people walk at about 2.5 mph, a bit too slow for maximum benefits. It's much better to maintain a pace of about 4 mph. This can be done by measuring the length of your course in advance (if along roads, use your car's odometer) and then ensuring that you complete each mile in about 15 minutes. This faster rate is not advisable when you're just beginning an exercise program, however; build up slowly to that pace to avoid risk of injury.

Another principle for walking, or any other aerobic activity you choose for enhancing your body's fat-burning capacity, involves the time of day that you train. Try doing your program in the morning, right after you roll out of bed and *before* you eat any breakfast. Or alternatively, work out late in the afternoon after school or work, when you haven't consumed any carbohydrates since lunch. Either approach is apt to enhance your fat-burning effort.

Regular walking, jogging, swimming, cycling, sports activities, or another of the many available forms of exercise is just as important for children as for adults. Studies show that barely half of America's young people (aged 10 to 18) are currently getting the minimum amount of exercise considered essential for a healthy heart. And there may be significant implications beyond the relationship of exercise to wellness. Consider that over 80 percent of young people who flunk out of college can't pass a minimum physical fitness test. Consider that most cadets who flunk out of the U.S. Naval Academy and Air Force Academy are at or near the bottom of their class in physical fitness.

The emerging message is that staying physically active *does* equate with doing better in school. One recent study of the effects of systematic physical training on the ability to perform mental work examined students in a boarding school where most factors of daily life, other than exercise, could be kept fairly constant. The findings clearly showed that the pupils who exercised far outdid their non-exercising counterparts in terms of mental work load.

At what age should children be encouraged into exercise activities? Again, this depends on their developmental stage and interests. But children between the ages of 6 and 10 are at the prime time of their lives for learning how to run faster. This can be stimulated in part through participation in games and activities that require acceleration (speed) and quick change of direction (agility). Such physical demands are found in jumping and running games like "leap-frog" and "jump-and-reach." These activities also help develop children's nervous systems.

Between the ages of 8 and 12, the refining of motor patterns (skill) and general coordination can be developed with activities requiring throwing and sprinting.

Overall, studies have found that most children who have not yet reached puberty can obtain many of the same cardiovascular benefits of endurance-type exercise as adults. And this cardiovascular toning is really important to the 25 percent of children who are obese.

But children who are obese often hate to exercise, especially if it is unpleasant or difficult due to their extra weight. Use an encouraging approach and let them select their own activity. Initially, it need not be intense. Once they have gained confidence, they can be encouraged to advance to more strenuous activities.

Again, I want to emphasize that the key with children is to *encourage* rather than push them into exercise programs and regular physical activity. As we've already learned, most attempts to "push" are counterproductive.

CHAPTER 18

Hazards Of Smoking

Highlights

✧ *Tobacco is now known to be the Number 1 cause of death in the U.S.*

✧ *Smoking has been linked to high blood pressure, heart disease, skeletal problems, various cancers, and other problems.*

✧ *Smoking also causes premature wrinkling of the face and male impotence.*

✧ *Current research links passive (secondhand) smoke to the same problems.*

✧ *At least 50 children's maladies have been linked to parental smoking.*

✧ *The good news is that quitting gradually reverses the risks to health caused by smoking.*

✧ *Each time you try to stop smoking, your chances of success increase.*

✧ *Sound motivational techniques, as given in this book, up your chance of quitting even more.*

In Part Two of this book, I talked about the need for both parents to avoid the abuse of alcohol, "hard" or "recreational" drugs, and cigarettes just before and during pregnancy. While research supporting the need for such precautions grows almost daily, for one of these maladies—smoking—the evidence of harmful effects is already quite overwhelming.

So why have tobacco products, which we now know are truly instruments of death, been literally studied to death? Think about it for a moment. Tobacco is a government-subsidized farm crop. It provides an economic base in certain regions and thus receives strong political support. Combine these factors with the tobacco products industry, a megabusiness with huge profits and political lobbying capacity, and it's no wonder researchers studying the harmful effects of tobacco products have been forced to prove and reprove their findings. Virtually every study which portrays smoking as harmful has been challenged and downplayed by the tobacco industry. Nevertheless, over time, important findings are being established and corroborated.

Today it is estimated that, of all the actual causes (i.e., the underlying *cause*, not the resulting disease) of death in this country, tobacco comes in a resounding Number 1. Tobacco's 400,000 deaths annually is the equivalent of three 747 jets full of passengers crashing every day of the year. Yet 30 to 40 million Americans continue to smoke, and expensive advertising campaigns to recruit new smokers continue around the clock.

We now know that smoking just a few cigarettes a day is enough to cause the vascular system to develop clots and lesions. Arteries may collect plaque that causes blockages. The tendency of blood to clot and form platelet clumps is hastened, and the good HDL cholesterol is reduced. The risk of seriously high blood pressure rises sharply because the nicotine in cigarettes even further constricts the already-affected blood vessels.

And the detrimental effects on the smoker's cardio-vascular system are definitely only the tip of the proverbial iceberg. New links of smoking with other serious diseases are being discovered almost weekly. For instance, a recent Centers for Disease Control and Prevention study found tobacco smoke as the cause for almost one-quarter of all cases of myeloid leukemia, making it the leading known cause of this deadly disease. Another study has concluded that the benefit of taking supplemental estrogen to prevent osteoporosis in older women literally goes up in smoke if they smoke.

A related study indicates that cigarette smoking may have a harmful effect (direct or indirect) on the health of the spine's intervertebral discs; in other words, smoking may literally cause a pain in the back, especially the lower back. Smoking is even known to dramatically increase the rate of breakdown of Vitamin C, which can result in deficiencies of this water-soluble nutrient. Vitamin C is essential for the production, maintenance, and healing of connective tissue such as intervertebral discs, hence chronic deficiencies could further exacerbate back problems.

> ## Some people will never live to be as old as they look.

Yet another new study has found a strong link between smoking and cervical cancer in women.

If making you susceptible to all kinds of ailments and deadly diseases isn't enough to dissuade you from this deadly habit, here are more facts. Smoking can even affect your appearance and sex life. Smoking has long been known to cause premature wrinkling of the face—including so-called "crow's feet." About a quarter of all longtime smokers experience this problem, but it is most prevalent in male smokers during their 50s.

The effect of smoking on sex lives was recently demonstrated by Boston University School of Medicine researchers and has been corroborated by others. The astonishing finding was that male smokers are four times more likely to become impotent than nonsmoking men. It turns out that smoking damages the blood vessels that initiate and sustain erections; it apparently also compounds a gradual loss of elasticity in the arteries, thus limiting blood flow to the penis.

But perhaps most astonishing of all is what has been learned over the last decade, and especially in the last 3 years, regarding "passive" smoke. This is the smoke we get secondhand when others smoke near us.

New scientific evidence shows passive smoke as far more harmful than ever imagined. According to University of California at San Francisco researchers, passive smoke is the third leading preventable cause of death in the U.S., killing an estimated 53,000 nonsmokers each year. Secondhand cigarette smoke has been classified as a "Group A carcinogen." But it's not cancer from the secondhand smoke that causes the most deaths; it's heart disease, the researchers say. They estimate that passive smoke causes 37,000 deaths a year from heart disease, compared to about 16,000 cancer deaths from secondhand smoke.

A recent study by an international team led by Harvard University researchers has provided the first direct medical evidence that secondhand smoke can damage the lungs of nonsmokers. The team autopsied nonsmoking women and found that the lungs of those whose husbands smoked had significantly more precancerous abnormalities than those whose husbands were nonsmokers. Previous studies based on statistical-only evidence of lung cancer rates in wives and children of smokers estimated about 4,000 deaths a year from cancer caused by secondhand smoke. But the tobacco industry argued that the reported link between cancer and secondhand smoke was based on biased epidemiological data. The latest studies corroborate the earlier statistics and refute the industry's counterargument.

One of the recent studies places a nonsmoking wife's cancer risk at 30 percent higher if she has a smoking husband, a risk that rises with the number of cigarettes he smokes and her years of exposure.

Similar increased risks of cancer related to other sources of passive smoke in adult life, such as at work and in social settings, are also being revealed. These risks are likely to be at least as great as those related to having a spouse who smokes. Again, of course, the findings run counter to the position of the Tobacco Institute—the official mouthpiece for the tobacco industry—which contends that the hazards of secondhand smoke outside of the home are greatly exaggerated.

What does all this mean in relation to children? Clearly, parents who smoke in the home may be planting long-term disease and behavioral time bombs in their children. Very young children are particularly susceptible because their immature respiratory and immune systems are less able to defend against the poison gases in environmental tobacco smoke.

A recent British study by doctors at Manchester University reviewed 143 scientific studies, spanning 20 years, into how children are affected by parents who smoke. More than 50 children's ailments and disorders were linked to the smoking. Some of the conditions, such as sore throats and eyes, sneezing, and coughs, are relatively minor. But others, including crib death, meningitis, cystic fibrosis, pneumonia, congenital heart disease, and later, vulnerability to cancer, are quite serious.

Strong evidence is also emerging of a passive smoking link to children's behavioral troubles. One study found that the more cigarettes a mother smoked, the more behavioral problems her children were likely to have. Women who smoked at least a pack a day had children with twice the rate of extreme behavioral problems—anxiety, hyperactivity, disobedience, antisocial behavior, or interpersonal conflicts— as the children of nonsmokers. Quite surprisingly, smoke exposure seems to be rivaling other major stresses on children (along with poverty, low birth weight, chronic illness, and parental divorce) as the cause of serious behavioral problems.

How can smoking possibly be related to such a wide range of problems? Consider that at least 600 to 700 ingredients are used in the manufacture of cigarettes alone. The tobacco industry must report these so-called "trade secrets" to the federal government. But the government is not allowed to reveal them to us; in fact, present law makes it a felony to do so. Nevertheless, both the ingredients and their dangers are gradually being revealed by various sources. For example, a recent story carried by the Reuters News Service claims that at least 13 of the chemicals being used in cigarettes are deemed too dangerous to be used in foods and "could not be dumped in a landfill under current environmental laws."

With so much bad news about smoking, is there *anything* good to report? The best news is that when smoking or exposure to passive smoke is halted, the health risks gradually reverse themselves. In one long-term landmark study of 121,700 female nurses which began in 1976, results showed that the statistical health risks 10 to 14 years after quitting smoking had returned to the same levels as for nonsmokers. The study also revealed that the benefits of quitting smoking were "clearly present regardless of the age at starting and daily number of cigarettes smoked" and that these benefits "begin to accrue almost immediately after quitting."

The dilemma is that breaking the smoking habit is an extremely difficult thing to do. The U.S. Surgeon General's 1988 report on smoking and health confirmed one of the main reasons why: Cigarette smoking is a very physically addictive habit caused by nicotine, a powerful substance in the cigarettes.

Scientists now say that nicotine affects levels of a brain chemical important to emotions called dopamine. Smokers very quickly fall into a trap where they need more and more nicotine to re-create the sensations caused by fluctuating dopamine levels.

> ## *Quitting smoking is easy.*
> ## *I've done it a thousand times.*

In 1988, then Surgeon General C. Everett Koop first officially tagged nicotine as cigarettes' addictive ingredient. But there is evidence that the tobacco industry knew of this potential hazard much sooner. For example, a recent Associated Press report says that a 1983 study by Phillip Morris Company, showing that nicotine was addictive in studies with rats, was twice withdrawn from publication in a prestigious scientific journal, thus effectively holding back knowledge by years.

Research into smoking cessation shows that persistence is one of the keys to success. Too often, smokers try one approach and it fails, so they give up. But, in fact, each time a smoker *tries* to quit, no matter what the approach, the overall *chances* are increased.

One school of thought is that quitting "cold turkey" is the best way. A newer view from addiction researchers at the University of California at San Diego says that "tapering off" may be better.

With this newer approach, those who can *delay* the day's first cigarette or give up smoking for 7 days have a good chance of eventually kicking the habit. Smokers are encouraged to make progress by smoking less and more intermittently, as opposed to the difficult choice of stopping immediately. A recent program in California based on this concept enabled over a quarter of the participants to give up smoking, roughly twice the percentage of those able to quit without the program. An apparently essential feature of the program, however, was repeated follow-up contacts from counselors.

Remember that regardless of the approach you choose to stop smoking, the single greatest determinant to success is your *motivation*. Use the principles and techniques discussed earlier in this book, particularly those in the Goals and Goal-Setting chapter and The Winning Attitude chapter to help you develop, focus, and maintain your motivation.

CHAPTER 19

Stress Reduction

Highlights

✧ *When exposed to stress, the body releases hormones that affect bodily functions, preparing it to "fight or take flight."*

✧ *Many debilitating ailments are triggered by too much stress.*

✧ *Control stress in your life by:*
  ✧ *acknowledging that stress is a normal part of life;*
  ✧ *learning to say "no" to gain control of your life;*
  ✧ *applying stress-busting tips;*
  ✧ *changing the way you think;*
  ✧ *exercising regularly, eating properly, and getting enough sound, restful sleep.*

✧ *Learn at least one deep relaxation method to help control stress.*

Stress inevitably affects each of us. The overall magnitude of its effects is illustrated by these statistics: 1) stress on the job results in over a half billion work days lost a year, ultimately costing U.S. industry more than $200 billion;

2) five out of six workers feel that job stress plays a major factor in their illnesses; 3) about 90 percent of American adults feel "high levels of stress" at least once a week, definitely making it a "disease" of our era.

Paul J. Rosch, head of the American Institute of Stress, defines this "disease" rather simply as "the sense or feeling of being out of control."

The body's natural, physiological response to stress comes from our distant evolutionary heritage and is called the "fight-or-flight response." When exposed to stress, the body naturally brews a hormonal "soup" that increases heart rate, blood pressure, metabolism, and blood flow to muscles. It temporarily shuts down certain bodily functions. It depresses the immune system. All of this evolved in our distant past to prepare us to either stand and make a fight, or to retreat quickly from harm's way.

> *Many people suffer poor health not because of what they eat but from what is eating them.*

Most problems arise when stress is unusually severe and prolonged. Constant heavy stress triggers all kinds of debilitating ailments. The hormonal soup brewing inside us without release causes diseases ranging from colds to heart attacks, creates numerous symptoms which mimic other diseases and medical conditions, skews our cholesterol count, lowers our scores on tests, and destroys our peace of mind and feelings of well-being. Below is a list of the more common warning signs of too much stress:

Physical Symptoms
   ✧ Headaches
   ✧ Indigestion
   ✧ Sweaty palms
   ✧ Sleep difficulty
   ✧ Dizziness
   ✧ Tight neck/shoulders
   ✧ Tiredness
   ✧ Restlessness

Behavioral Changes
   ✧ Excessive smoking
   ✧ Bossiness
   ✧ Overeating
   ✧ Alcohol overuse
   ✧ Destructive criticism
      against others
   ✧ Compulsive gum
      chewing

Emotional Signs
   ✧ Cry easily
   ✧ Bored
   ✧ Anxious
   ✧ Easily upset
   ✧ Unhappy
   ✧ Nervous
   ✧ Feelings of powerlessness

Thought Symptoms
   ✧ Forgetfulness
   ✧ Constant worry
   ✧ No creativity
   ✧ Unclear thinking
   ✧ Memory loss
   ✧ Inability to make
      decisions

Obviously, stress can bring about some serious consequences, and controlling stress is often a major prerequisite to achieving success as individuals.

An important first step in controlling stress is to acknowledge and understand that it's a part of everyday life. You can control it to some degree, but you'll never make it go away altogether, so don't waste your time trying.

You can only do good if you feel good.

Another helpful tactic is learning to say "No." Many of life's stresses come from feeling overburdened and out of control. Learning to say no to your children, spouse, boss, friends, and others can reduce the burden and make you feel better.

Here are 10 more good stress-busting tips compiled from a number of expert sources:

- ✧ Write a nasty letter to whoever is stressing you out, then simply tear it up.
- ✧ Volunteer to do something worthwhile. You'll feel better knowing who you are and that there are others worse off than yourself.
- ✧ Unplug the phone, send the family to a movie, and listen to some favorite music.
- ✧ Don't be afraid of tears. Sometimes a good cry is called for; it can release tension.
- ✧ Accept yourself. Don't expect to be perfect all the time; some things don't *have* to be done perfectly.
- ✧ Take a warm bath or play with a pet.
- ✧ Set a comfortable, steady pace at work, then focus on the task at hand to improve productivity.
- ✧ Schedule some time for fun; it's as vital as work.
- ✧ Avoid using caffeine-containing drinks to excess. Caffeine is an adrenaline enhancer. It can worsen the symptoms of and body responses to stress. Avoid excess tobacco and alcohol for the same reasons.
- ✧ Confide in a close friend. Having true friends to whom you can speak freely without fear of criticism is important.

There are also a number of positive actions centered on the way we *think* that will help reduce stress. These were discussed in detail earlier in The Winning Attitude chapter. This is a good time to go back and reread that chapter or its Hightlights. Rereading the chapter on goal-setting may also be beneficial at this time.

Exercise should also be a part of any stress-reduction effort. Follow the guidelines I discussed in Chapter 17 and put yourself onto a regular exercise regime. One of the effects of exercise and working the heart is to help the heart muscle metabolize excess adrenaline. As the adrenaline is used up, the heart rate slows, and some of the other symptoms caused by too much stress subside.

In fact, exercise seems to "inoculate" us against stress, researchers from Arizona State University have found. Aerobically fit people have a reduced "psychosocial stress response," apparently "because exercise itself stresses the body." Thus, "repeated exercise (the inoculations) may increase the exerciser's capacity for dealing with stress in all forms," the researchers explain.

Considerable evidence that exercise profoundly affects the brain has been compiled. Exactly how is still open to debate, however. Scientists do know that part of the benefits may be attributable to morphine-like chemical receptors called endogenous opioids. The blood level of one opioid, called B-endorphin, increases during exercise.

Another theory is that exercise, by raising the body's core temperature, enhances levels of chemicals called neurotransmitters in the brain, and these may elevate mood and ease depression. Others suggest that electrical tension in muscles is reduced by exercise, or exercise enhances the transport of oxygen to the brain.

Regardless of the exact cause and effect, it is clear that a regular exercise program is beneficial in reducing stress. There are also some "on-the-spot" exercises that can help you deal directly with upcoming stressful events (such as giving a speech) that may be making you nervous and tense; these exercises can also help you deal with tedious or monotonous work, such as typing or keypunching. Here are three on-the-spot exercise techniques that may be effective for you:

1. **Shoulder shrugs:** Hold the "shrug" position about 3 seconds, then relax. Repeat these shrugs for 3 minutes.
2. **Neck rolls:** Slowly tilt your head to the side, lower it forward, then tilt it to the other side. Do these about 3 minutes too, while breathing deeply.

3. **Fist clenches:** Squeeze your fists tightly for 3 seconds, then relax. Repeat for about 3 minutes.

Regular exercise isn't the only answer to stress control, however. Another essential part of the equation is proper diet. Focus on the type of wholesome foods diet and general prudent eating habits I discussed earlier. Despite today's well-publicized fitness movement, many people are still unaware of how important their diets are to their emotional stability and handling of everyday stress.

In considering diet effects on emotional health, an important chemical to pay attention to is serotonin. Synthesized within the body from L-tryptophan, an essential amino acid, serotonin is a neurotransmitter. When serotonin is lacking, all sorts of problems can develop, from irritability, frustration, sadness, and apathy to sleeping disorders, anxiety disorders, and even full-blown depression. It's important to eat tryptophan-rich foods from which the body synthesizes serotonin. Foods high in tryptophan include turkey, chicken, red meat (*limit* this one for other health reasons), seafood, and various nuts and seeds. People with mild emotional problems may find that tryptophan-rich diets are all they need to control the situation.

Along with a proper diet and exercise regime, it is essential to get a normal amount of sleep—sound, restful sleep—to successfully combat stress. Unfortunately, this is often more easily said than done. In a stressed-out condition, we're apt to either sleep too much or not enough (i.e., unable to fall asleep or waking up and being unable to return to sleep).

If such difficulties arise, there are certain do's and dont's. First, avoid using sleeping pills or antihistamines that can also make you drowsy. They significantly reduce REM (Rapid Eye Movement) sleep, a critical component of the nightly sleep cycle. Also avoid caffeine, nicotine, and large meals at night, especially close to bedtime; they make it all the more difficult for you to get to sleep.

If you have trouble sleeping one night, don't sleep late

the next morning. That only makes you more likely to have trouble getting to sleep the next night, perpetuating the cycle. In other words, try to maintain your regular sleeping pattern and times.

> ### Early to bed and early to rise makes a man healthy, wealthy, and wise.

When you go to bed, try the autosuggestion technique used by many Russian athletes. It works like this: First, recite some relaxation affirmations, such as "My body is getting relaxed" or "My legs are getting warm" or "My hands are getting relaxed." Then silently in your mind repeat the following affirmative "sleep formula" several times or until you fall asleep:

1. I *want* to sleep.
2. My eyelids are getting heavy.
3. My eyes are themselves closing.
4. My sleep will be calm and peaceful.
5. Eight hours (or whatever *your* magic number is) of sleep will totally refresh me.
6. I will wake up at 7 o'clock (or whatever *your* time is).
7. I am falling asleep, falling asleep...

If your sleep problem involves nightmares, especially the kind that center around a recurring theme, here's an effective solution from a recent issue of *Science*: Write down the gist of the nightmare with the added twist of how you *want* it to turn out. Then sit quietly and visualize this ideal scenario at least once a day for 3 days. That's all there is to it!

Besides a healthy lifestyle, which includes sleeping, eating, and exercising properly, the other single most powerful tool we have for dealing with stress is deep relaxation. Buddhist monks and yogis learned the benefits of calming the body with such methods thousands of years ago.

Everyone can benefit from relaxing deeply each day. If you don't think you have the time, make it. A daily regime of relaxation effectively dissipates many of the negative effects of stress, leaving your body physically and emotionally refreshed and rejuvenated.

The main prerequisite for applying a deep relaxation method is to do it in a quiet place. This may mean a darkened room in your house or perhaps a secluded place you can drive to in your car. Wherever the site selected, the environmental "noise" should be kept to a minimum.

Deep relaxation can be approached in a number of ways. Formal processes, such as yoga, meditation, or biofeedback, can be applied. Or you can tailor a less formal method to your own tastes, using the common components. I discussed **autogenic conditioning** in earlier chapters in relation to visualizing goals and reawakening creativity. Two expanded variations of autogenic conditioning are described below. Experiment with each technique to find out which one works better for you in providing stress relief. Or alternatively, seek instruction in one of the more formal procedures.

Technique 1: Start by loosening any tight clothing. Recline on your back, separating your legs so that the thighs do not touch. Extend your arms out slightly from the body with the palms facing downward and the fingers spread apart.

Remain as still as possible and fix your eyes on a spot above you. Now, take a few deep breaths, exhaling slowly through your mouth. As you exhale the last breath, slowly close your eyes. For the next dozen or so breaths, mentally repeat the word "calm" as you exhale. Gently push any distractions out of your mind as you repeat the word "calm."

After a dozen or so "calming" breaths, focus on relaxing the muscles of each body part. Start with your toes and move up through your legs, thighs, and so on, all the way to your face and the top of your head. As you focus on these parts, concentrate on letting them relax completely. Try thinking of them becoming loose rubber bands and "feel" the deep relaxation flowing to the muscles with each easy breath. You'll soon be experiencing the serenity that comes with total body relaxation.

Technique 2: Use the same starting procedure as in technique 1. Lie comfortably on your back, fix your eyes on a point above, and take a few slow, deep breaths (exhaling through your mouth).

After closing your eyes, focus on relaxing them so completely that you feel you wouldn't be able to open them if you wanted to. You might imagine your eyelids are window shades pulled down tightly and tacked to the window sill, so they can't be retracted. Begin repeating mentally the word "release" each time you exhale, while allowing your eyelids to get heavier and heavier against the window sill. When you think you've relaxed your eyelids to the point they can't be opened, try it and confirm that you've been successful.

Next, while keeping the "release" thought going in combination with the slow breathing, shift your thoughts to your hands. Visualize them as made of lead or stone and begin to "feel" their heaviness. Focus on this until you feel the increased weight and a tingling sensation in your fingertips.

Finally, imagine yourself at the top of a grand staircase which has 10 steps. At the bottom of the staircase is the most profound, deep relaxation level possible. As you descend down each step in your mind, let go of a little more and drift down toward that level. Mentally count yourself down: nine—I'm going *deeper* down; eight—I'm going *deeper* down; and so on, until you reach the last step. By then, you'll be feeling a profound sense of serene relaxation.

With either Technique 1 or 2, once you've become deeply relaxed, begin to visualize in your mind a scene that for you represents total tranquility and peace. It may be a beach scene with white sand, swaying palm trees, and gently rolling, aquamarine waters. Or it could be a beautiful forest with birds singing and sunlight filtering through the trees, reflecting off a crystal clear stream.

Pick a scene that truly appeals to you. Then move yourself mentally into that environment. Hear the sounds, smell the smells, see the sights, and feel the warmth of the sun or gentle brush of the breeze. Do this for about 10 minutes, then slowly open your eyes and return to your "real" physical environment. But don't get up for 5 minutes or so.

This kind of "trip" spent relaxing in your mind's ideal environment daily should easily be enough to diminish the debilitating effects of your everyday stresses.

APPENDIX:

Stories From Which Children (And Adults) Can Learn And Grow

Acres Of Gold

The storekeeper had made a good life for himself. His wife loved him, his three sons grew up, married nice young women and had children of their own. Everyone was thriving.

The store he ran was in a small town in Colorado. All the prospectors who flocked to the high mountains around the town searching for gold bought their supplies in his general store. The storekeeper kept investing his money over the years and, soon he owned a quarter of all the buildings in town as well as much of the land around it.

But the storekeeper was restless. The newspapers were full of stories about the newest gold rush in California. The papers said miners were getting fabulously rich in just weeks, some in only days, if they struck the mother lode. The storekeeper got really excited when he read about how much gold was being found in California, much more than had ever been discovered around his small town.

So he sold his buildings and land, told his wife to put on her hat and pack the buggy, and off they went to follow his dreams in California.

The storekeeper didn't do as well in this gold rush. One of his partners stole all the gold they'd dug out of the ground, another man jumped his claim, and his wife died of disappointment or loneliness, or maybe both.

Old and broke, the man ended up begging for pennies on the streets in San Francisco. His dreams were gone, and so was his wealth.

Meanwhile, back in the little town in Colorado, his cousin Daniel, who had bought the store from him, was raising his own family and enjoying life. One day he said to his wife, "If I pick enough blackberries off those bushes out back, will you make a pie?"

His wife agreed so he took a small pail, walked out to the back of the lot where blackberry vines covered the ground, and began to pick. The biggest, juiciest berry of all slipped through his fingers, and as Daniel stooped to pick it up, he noticed that the rock looked golden.

Daniel pushed the vines aside and saw more rocks with that same golden shine. He got so excited that he knocked over the pail of berries. He cleared all the vines away and found a surface vein of pure gold, hidden all those years by the blackberry vines.

Sadly, the storekeeper who sold him the building had gone off to make his fortune without looking first in his own backyard.

Lessons

✧ **Start your search for new opportunities in your own backyard.**

✧ **Focus first within your own area(s) of excellence.**

✧ **Look for your "acres of gold" to be disguised as something else.**

Working By The Hour

The hurricane had blown in from the Gulf of Mexico, knocking down dozens of power poles and miles of lines. Much of the city was without electricity.

Bill took his crew of six linemen to repair the lines in the southern part of the city. As they worked in the hot sun, safely tethered to their poles, Bill and the other linemen noticed a fancy new car pull up to the curb. A man in a gray suit with a red silk tie climbed from the back seat of the car and looked up at the men working on the lines. It was the company president.

"Hello, Bill," he shouted. "How are the repairs coming?"

"Well, John," Bill called down to him, "there's a lot more damage than we thought, but we should have the lights back on by tomorrow morning."

Lunchtime came and the men climbed down from the poles, took their lunch boxes from the utility truck, and sat on the curb to eat.

"There are 3,000 people who work for this company," Jeff said to Bill between giant bites of his sandwich. "How come the president of the company knows your name?"

"Well," Bill said, "we both started out together as linemen for the company 28 years ago this month."

"And how is it," the lineman said after another bite, "that he made it to the top of the company while you're still just a lineman?"

"Because 28 years ago this month John went to work *for the company*, and I went to work for $1.69 per hour," was the reply.

Lessons

✧ **Giving more than you're paid for assures that you'll eventually be paid more for what you do.**

✧ **You can get everything in life you want by giving as many people as you can what they want.**

✧ **In every field, the top people are always assured of jobs.**

When The Going Gets Rough, Look Where You Want To Go

The storm had battered and tossed the old sailing ship for days. It was Josh's turn to climb up the rigging and undo the lines so that the sail could be changed.

This was Josh's first sea voyage, and he was frightened. The farther up the mast he climbed, the more the ship seemed to pitch and roll. His stomach felt like it was trying to roll in the opposite direction. Josh clung to the rigging and looked down at the deck far below. He was sure he would never get back down off the mast.

James, who had been in plenty of storms like this, stood on deck waiting for Josh to loosen the sail. "Look up, Josh," he yelled and pointed with his hand. "Just look up!"

Josh couldn't believe what the old salt was telling him. He stared down at the deck, afraid to move. But James kept yelling, "Look up!"

So finally Josh did. As he looked up at the stormy sky, his queasiness went away. "That's better," he said as he untied the ropes holding the sail. He then climbed easily back down to the safety of the deck below.

Lessons

✧ **When things appear bad, look forward and upward to where you want to be.**

✧ **Focus on what you desire, not what you fear.**

Give It Your Best Shot

Many years ago a man arrived in this country from Germany. He had lots of energy and enthusiasm but very little money and no job.

Instead of looking for a job that would pay him a small amount every hour he worked, the man put on his suit and walked into the biggest building on the street.

"I'll sell your widgets," he said, "and you don't have to give me wages. Just give me 10 cents for every widget I sell." He told them that he wanted to work for them because he knew they were on the way to the top.

"All I need is the title of vice president and some business cards with my name and title on them," he told the president of the company. "And I'll sell all the widgets you can make."

The president looked at the man in his clean white shirt with his plain tie carefully tied. "I like your ambition," he said. "The cards will be ready tomorrow."

The rest of the story is pure Horatio Alger. The man went to every big city and sold widgets. The company had a hard time making enough widgets to fill all the orders. The monthly commissions kept getting bigger and bigger. Soon the man was wearing expensive suits with silk ties and driving a fancy new car.

Lessons

✧ Use innovative approaches to get the job you want.

✧ Be willing to pay whatever price is necessary to get the job you want.

✧ Think of what you can give to get what you want.

✧ Make your appearance that of a winner.

Sleeping When The Wind Blows

When his son went away to college, Farmer Brown decided that he'd have to hire an extra hand to help run the farm. He asked the first young man who came to apply for the job, "What special talent do you have?"

The young man answered, "I can sleep when the wind blows."

His answer puzzled the farmer. But the young man looked strong, and maybe he was shy. Surely he had special talents. Farmer Brown went ahead and hired him.

His intuition proved correct. The young man came to work every day on time and worked hard till the end of the day.

Then one night there was a terrific storm with lots of rain and wind. Farmer Brown ran to the young man's room and banged on the door. "Henry," he shouted. "I need help with the animals." No answer came from behind the closed door. Finally, in a huff, the farmer threw on his rain gear and ran out into the storm to take care of the animals by himself.

What he found surprised him. The haystacks were covered and securely tied down. The animals were all inside with plenty of fresh food and water.

Then suddenly, the young man's earlier words—"I can sleep when the wind blows"—popped into the farmer's head.

"So that's what he meant," he said to the pig, who was the only animal with its eyes open, and nodded his head. The farmer returned to the house, took off his wet clothes, and climbed back into bed.

Lessons

✧ **Think of the obstacles in the path to your goals and prepare for them.**

✧ **Relieve your stress by taking action.**

✧ **Instill confidence, independence, and feelings of self-respect in your children to prepare them for life's experiences.**

Using What You Have

Mrs. Goodman's second grade class at Lemon Hill School had a problem. One of the three mice that the children had been observing since Christmas had escaped from its cage and was hiding somewhere in the classroom.

Each day the children looked and looked. But no one could find the missing mouse. It was very small and very hard to see.

Then Mrs. Goodman had an idea. "Stevie, will you please come to my desk," she said on the third morning. Stevie sat up straight in his seat when he heard his name, then walked carefully to the teacher's desk.

"Class," Mrs. Goodman said, "Stevie can find our mouse because he has a special talent. But you all must be very quiet."

And she was right. Stevie's talent was listening. He listened very carefully because he was blind. He let his ears tell him what was happening around him. Everyone stayed very quiet, and the mouse was soon back in the cage with its brother and sister.

The whole class clapped their hands as Stevie returned to his seat. He was delighted to put his special talent to use.

Years later, Stevie still remembered finding the mouse. "It was a real turning point in my life," he told a reporter who was interviewing him to write a story about the by-then famous songwriter and singer, Stevie Wonder.

Lessons

✧ Use your area(s) of excellence to win your goals.

✧ Encouragement offers more than discouragement or destructive criticism.

✧ Elevate performances—your own and those of others— by elevating your expectations.

Big Trucks And Little Boys

Many of our nation's railroad overpasses were built long before trucks began carrying cargo across the country. The more there was to carry, the bigger the trucks got. That's why more than one modern "big-rig" has become stuck under these sometimes-too-low overpasses.

It's said that this story really happened. A truck became stuck under an overpass, and everything the driver and police tried to free it didn't work. The truck stayed stuck.

A small boy on the sidewalk watched with interest. After two tow trucks tried to pull the big truck free and couldn't, he walked up to the policeman in charge.

"Mister, I know how to get it loose," said the boy.

"Son, you'd better stay back. You might get hurt," the policeman said and motioned him back to the sidewalk.

A bulldozer tried pushing the truck out from under the overpass, but it couldn't. Everyone stood around scratching their heads and wondering what to do next. Finally, the little boy, who was still standing on the sidewalk, shouted, "Just let some air out of the tires!"

All the adults who had been trying to figure out what to do next looked at each other sheepishly. In a few minutes the truck was free and on its way.

Lessons

✧ Learn to *listen* to your child and show respect for his or her ideas.

✧ The more you support your child's creative thinking, the more it will blossom.

You Learn What You're Taught

Mr. McDonald, teacher at Valley Elementary School, knows his lesson plans by heart. He should; he's been teaching first grade at the same school for 31 years.

Today, on the first day of class, Mr. McDonald tells the class that they are going to draw a picture. Mikey is excited; he likes to draw pictures, and so he begins immediately. Then Mr. McDonald says, "Today we will learn to draw a flower. Please watch how I do it on the board before you begin."

Mikey can't stop himself. The crayons are there. He has a clean piece of paper in front of him. He begins to draw flowers of every color. Mr. McDonald comes over to him, takes the crayon from his hand, and shows Mikey how to make a proper flower—red, with a green stem.

This lesson is followed by many others in which Mr. McDonald very patiently and carefully shows the children how to do each activity. Mikey learns the lessons well. He always waits, watches, and does things just like the teacher. And he gradually stops drawing his own pictures.

After Christmas, Mikey's family moves. He has to go to a new school hundreds of miles away. On the first day at the new school, the teacher tells the class to draw a picture, so Mikey waits for her to show him how. But she doesn't say anything more. She just walks around the room. Finally, she asks Mikey why he isn't drawing a picture.

"What should I draw?" asks Mikey.

"Draw anything you want," she says. So Mikey picks up a red crayon and draws a flower. Then he picks up the green crayon and draws a stem.

Lessons

✧ **Avoid showing your child how everything should be done.**

✧ **When a child shows you a creative product, find something in it to sincerely praise.**

✧ **You don't get more achievement by tightening the screws.**

Notes

Notes

Notes

Notes

Order Form

ORDERED BY:

Name: _____

Address: _____

City: _____ State: _____ Zip Code:_____

Telephone *(optional)*: (_____) _____

SEND TO *(if different than above)*:

Name: _____

Address: _____

City: _____ State: _____ Zip Code:_____

BOOK ORDER:

_____ Books @ $13.00* each   = $_____

   + $2.00 s/h *(first copy)*   = $_____

   + $1.00 s/h *(each addit'l. copy)*   = $_____

   + tax *(CA residents)*   = $_____

                 Total   = $_____

Additional copies on the same order are just $10.50 each. Further quantity discounts are also available for educational purposes. On your letterhead, include information as to number of books desired and intended use.

METHOD OF PAYMENT:

❏ Check Enclosed   ❏ Visa   ❏ MasterCard

Card No.: __ __ __ __ - __ __ __ __ - __ __ __ __ - __ __ __ __

Expiration Date: _____

Name on Card: _____

Signature: _____

SEND THIS FORM TO:
MayaLand Press, Dept. A, P.O. Box 1260, Davis, CA 95617, or for credit card orders, telephone or fax (916) 756-6200.